"Vital reading for surviving life-changing challenges."

IT COULD BE YOU...

Handbook for Real People
& Policymakers

PENNY MELVILLE-BROWN

ISBN: 978-1-7397990-1-4

Editor: Kimberley Miller at www.morethan-words.com

Interior design and publication: Clint MacDonald at www.mac-nificent.co.uk

Cover design: Alice Kennedy at www.glow-designs.co.uk

The punctuation may seem quirky but works with the screen-reader used by many visually impaired people.

Dedication.

For my beloved beekeeper husband and sensational sous-chef, Alan, plus everyone who generously gave their help, ideas and words to this venture: Andrew, Angela, Carol, Chris, Christina, Darren, David (several), Grant, Ian, John (both), Julie, Karen, Kimberley, Louise, Martin, Matt, Natalie, Nichola, Nick, Nicky, Paul (both), Peter, Richard, Rob, Sally (both), Simon, Stephen (both), Steve (both), Tim, Trevor, Victoria.

Acknowledgements.

My thanks to Kimberley Miller (editing and proofreading) of www.morethan-words.com and her team of Alice (cover) and Clint (typesetting plus Toby Melville-Brown) cover graphics) of www.tobymelvillebrown.com who all brought their respective skills to the publication of this book.

Contents List.

"After years delivering disability training, I'm humbly sure that, rather than the outstandingly wonderful content, success was due to the groups' realisation that I was just like them: enthusiastic but fallible; professional but human."

Penny

CHAPTER 1.

Apologies.

Sorry if you got this book in the hope of winning the lottery and getting rich quick! But reading on could still be life-changing.

I remember that, when it was first created, the odds of winning the new National Lottery were about 14 million to 1. This book is about disability and, before you put it down, your chances of being one of us are much higher: about 1-in-4 (if you're working, with extra increases in the early 40s and 60s), and higher after retirement. There's even been a recent surge amongst young people. All of this makes disabled people the largest 'minority' but, perhaps, without enough of the right sort of public attention.

Almost inevitably, the life of each disabled person changes that of at least one other. There are:

- All the families, friends and informal carers.
- Everyone involved in healthcare, including all those providing care, nursing and hospice facilities.
- Untold numbers of politicians and government officials delivering our benefits, education, support, employment, transport services and much more.
- Those across the business and voluntary sectors.
- Everyone serving the public, employing anyone, and even landlords have specific responsibilities.

From 1-in-4, disability easily plays a part in the lives of *vast* numbers of the population.

Gentle reader, it is far more likely that you will be affected by disability than ever winning that jackpot.

16 to 64-year-olds

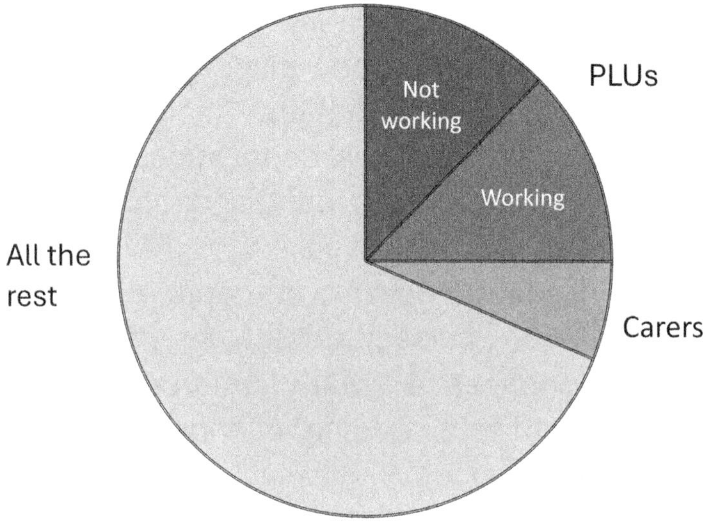

But good news: having a life-changing health condition needn't be the end of the world. The following pages reveal possible ways of tackling, and overcoming, some of our challenges. Take a stroll with me through 25 years of learning.

Forgive me, as I'm still not an expert on every aspect of disability. The pages ahead probably focus too much on sight loss, because it's what I know. Others have their own invaluable different insights and knowledge, such as those within the deaf community, with conditions since birth or childhood, or with multiple complex interlinked conditions. Unlike some, I didn't have to face the trauma of sudden onset, accident, violence or conflict, but, like many, just slid into middle age and deteriorating health. There are other challenges too, such as deprivation, location, education, ethnic background and more.

It's impossible to cover every topic, nuance or consequence of disability. But using the voices and experiences of many others (including those named in the Dedication) hopefully offers a broader perspective.

Trying to avoid too many figures throughout, rather than percentages, I've rounded numbers up and down. Facts and figures aren't written in stone but can be fluid with time and should be taken with a pinch of salt. (Even the illustrious Office for National Statistics (ONS) Labour Force Survey (LFS) data seems to have been less than reliable during the post-Covid years.)

The data comes from various sources, and I commend the ONS report on "Outcomes for Disabled People" (2022). The England and Wales Census (2021) has been important but, of course, didn't cover Scotland or Northern Ireland. The government's "Getting Britain Working" White Paper (2024), the follow-up "Pathways to Work" Green Paper (2025), and other illustrious sources, including the Joseph Rowntree and Resolution Foundations (JRF and RF), have all been invaluable.

I've tried not to be political, but that doesn't mean not being critical of the situation we face. Back in the early years of this millennium, I was involved in a government disability project. "Equality 2025" was the goal – and now would have been the time – but some utterly forgettable minister allegedly for disabled people let the initiative fade. We are still waiting.

The United Nations Committee on the Convention on the Rights of Persons with Disabilities offers an international perspective and raises a red flag. We signed up to the Convention in 2009 and, despite various reviews, still receive criticism. Their report talked of *"no significant progress"* and even *"grave and systematic violations of the human rights of persons with disabilities and has failed to eliminate the root causes of inequality and discrimination"*, particularly in relation to the right to *"live independently and be included in the community, to work and employment, and to an adequate standard of living and social protection"* (2024). 'Could do better' seems to be their general opinion.

Warning.

Before even more economic or international stresses arise, remember the 1904 Fitzroy Report raising alarm about the poor physical condition of UK army recruits for the Boer War. That high level of national risk continues if we don't constantly nurture every human resource available.

Finally, while writing this, I got thoroughly fed up with phrases like 'disabled people' and 'people with disabilities'. I'm one of them and so are, potentially, many of you readers, so meet 'People Like Us', shortened to PLUs, the *real people* behind the 'disability' label.

So what?

If you're 16+, there is a 1-in-4 chance you'll be a PLUs too, and the odds get higher after 65.

CHAPTER 2.

Who are we?

On just one day: the King's cancer; failed pelvic meshes; children damaged by their mothers' epilepsy medication; queues for NHS dental treatment; companies hiding the unhealthiness of their junk food; thousands injured in Gaza; a surge of mental health conditions amongst young people.

When you're tuned in to PLUs, you find we're everywhere! And the numbers are probably higher than you'd think. For example:

- Comments about the King's treatment suggested that 1-in-2 of us will have cancer sometime in our lives, and that there's been a global increase amongst the under-50s, lifestyle and diet changes being amongst the prime suspects (2024).
- About a quarter of 16-64-year-olds (loosely, 'working age') in the UK are PLUs, and even more amongst the 65+s (2024).

> *"Other people couldn't see that I was ill, so they didn't understand because I look as fit as anyone else. I ended up on benefits: I was ashamed of not being able to support my family as the illness had stripped away everything."* (Anon)

The law.

Let's get some basics over. The Equality Act 2010 says a person has a disability if they have *"a physical or mental impairment and that impairment has a substantial and long-term adverse effect on their ability to carry out normal day-to-day activities"* (Section 6).

Rather a mouthful. It makes more sense when broken down into bits: 'substantial' usually means more than minor; 'long term' usually means has or is likely to last 12 months or until death; 'normal day-to-day activities' might include using a stepladder to change a lightbulb, but perhaps not teetering atop a chimney! Simple: these are health conditions that are life-changing.

Not every condition has to prove every part of the definition. Diagnosis alone is enough for cancer, HIV infection and multiple sclerosis to be disabilities, while a consultant ophthalmologist's certification of blind, severely sight impaired, or partially sighted/ sight impaired, works too. There's masses more government guidance online.

In contrast, most addictions are outside the definition, along with hay-fever and sight loss corrected by glasses or contact lenses.

The big picture.

In 2021, England and Wales hit their highest population numbers since 1801 according to the Census. There were some expected trends: the number of over-65s had shot up by 2 million (nearly 1-in-5) since 2011; women outnumbered men; inward migration had contributed. Covid and other life factors were also playing their part. Lives and health were more difficult due to the 'cost-of-living crisis' making food expensive and homes colder. The World Health Organisation (WHO) was despairing of the damage caused by ultra-processed food, alcohol, tobacco and fossil fuels, while the levels of microplastics in our bodies were raising questions too. Other conditions, such as menopause, were being recognised as potentially disabling.

PLUs and age.

It's easy to assume that passing years are a key driver of life-changing conditions. But it's not the only cause and nor is it about 'old age' and 'retirement'. In fact, about half of us PLUs gained our conditions before retirement to produce that quarter of working-age people.

Children.

Thankfully, fewer than 1-in-10 under-15-year-olds were counted as PLUs (2021), but the numbers may have been skewed. During the previous decade, the number of 10-24-year-old PLUs had doubled to 1.2 million. Many needed help for conditions such as anxiety, depression, autism and ADHD. Diagnoses may have improved but varied in consistency, NHS appointments/treatments were sometimes slow, and local councils had problems handling all the school Special Educational Needs and Disability (SEND) assessment applications. By 2024, over 400,000 children had been waiting years for the diagnosis, treatment and help they needed according to the Children's Commissioner.

> *"I'd been run over when I was 16 and my leg was smashed from top to bottom," David explained. "I'd been doing upholstery for my whole career until I took redundancy when I had to have my damaged knee replaced, plus other operations on my hands and shoulders. I'm in constant pain from the silent illness, fibromyalgia."*

Young adults.

Just over 1-in-10 were PLUs in 2021, with some increase possibly caused by the pandemic lockdowns and social isolation. The Census had also caught up with the law and asked, for the first time, about mental health on top of the usual physical conditions. This may have been one reason for higher responses, especially amongst young people. Nearly a third of 18-24-year-olds were reporting mental disorder symptoms such as depression, anxiety or bipolar disorder (2021-22). Alongside,1-in-7 women in their 20s had mental health conditions due to sexual, physical and coercive abuse.

> *Natalie described her family tragedies: "My mother passed away when I was 12 and my father died four years later. I was then in foster care before living alone. My first marriage was very abusive and I lost my baby due to the violence when I was pregnant. Afterwards, I was hospitalised for mental health treatment. I'm now much happier and my health is better," Natalie said. "I had worked with other young people who, like me, had to learn to live independently. But it was very depressing when I wasn't able to work because of my illness."*

Smartphones, social media and algorithms were also being blamed by some for their impact on mental health for, perhaps, the previous decade. Strikingly, there were more self-declarations by young people in America too. Having such conditions may have become more socially acceptable. Looking to the future, more 25-34-year-old PLUs also weren't working, with all the associated, potentially lifelong financial consequences.

Middle age.

PLUs made up about 2-in-10 of 40-50-year-olds and the levels were higher by pension age (2021). Likewise, earning power got more difficult with those passing years. The result was over half the out of work PLUs were aged 50-64 (2022) with possible pension impact still to come.

> *After leaving the Royal Navy, Trevor had been crushed in a building site accident. "I had a broken pelvis and lots of muscle damage. My mobility was limited and, as I'm getting older, arthritis is setting in. I did try lots of different jobs but couldn't manage full days of heavy work. Not being able to work during the last few years got me down in the dumps and frustrated." But he still managed to work. "Running the business has made me much happier as I'm working without pain and making an income rather than being on benefits. The work helps my wife too as it reduces her high blood pressure condition. Our son is thrilled that we are making such a success."*

Pension age.

Surprisingly, the 2021 Census seemed to show more than a million fewer PLUs over-60s. Again, the pandemic may have been a cause. Pressure on the NHS may have reduced or delayed PLUs-by-diagnosis, and those already vulnerable (especially in care homes) may not have survived. But part of the cause may have been simpler. In 2011, the previous Census had prompted us to 'include problems related to old age'. Ticking the box may have been easier when the disability label seemed more socially and emotionally acceptable. It probably wasn't a coincidence that, when the prompt was dropped, the response rates did too. Those planning and financing future health and social care may need to treat the figures with caution.

Risk points.

There are indicators that health deteriorates at specific times in life for some: mid-40s; around 60; late-70s.

Education.

Most finish school and other education well before the typical middle-age and later onset of disability. But it seemed that less learning success and fewer qualifications were a marker for future disability. Although there's been some improvement, compared with others, working-age PLUs were:

- Three times more likely to have no qualifications (even higher for 55-64-year-olds).
- More likely to have no qualifications above GCSEs.
- Less likely to have university degrees (about a quarter compared with over 4-in-10 of others), with young PLUs not matching the general increase at universities.
- A rather startling Israeli study even linked *"lower cognitive performance in adolescence and an increased risk of early-onset stroke"* (2024).

Reading ages.

Just a note of caution: don't muddle 'reading ages' with brain power, intelligence or potential.

> *Dyslexic Sir Richard became a multi-billionaire, and Steve regularly requalifies as an outstanding heating engineer thanks to a bit more time and print on coloured background.*

For others, vocabulary grounded in Norman-French and Latin woven into those complex, multi-clause sentences so beloved of civil servants can cause most problems. Writing in the Anglo-Saxon we still speak can be clearer.

> *When I was working with HMRC, we were advised to write for the national average reading age: that of 11-year-olds. Tabloid newspapers aimed at 9-year-olds and the broadsheets at 14!*

There are practical consequences to this: 3-in-5 people couldn't read health instructions well enough to do what was needed according to one study.

Location counts.

PLUs aren't spread evenly around the country. For example, the population in parts of the north-east and Wales, such as Blackpool, Blaenau Gwent and Neath Port Talbot, had the highest levels of PLUs. The lowest levels were in London and the south-east, dipping down to about 1-in-10 in London (2021). Later numbers underlined the difference: generally, boys born in 2022 could expect to live until 80 with 63 years of healthy life. While those were the averages, the difference between those in the richest and poorest areas was much starker: 10 years different life expectancy and 19 years difference in healthy life (ONS, 2024). If the prospect is a shorter, unhealthier life from birth, the future is already looking bleak.

People in the poorest and richest areas reach the same level of disability but with 30 years difference. Breaking those poverty cycles is tough when so many years of work and earning are at high risk.

Multiple deprivation.

Governments used the seven Indices of Multiple Deprivation (IMD) in the neighbourhoods of England's local council areas (2004-19). Those neighbourhoods ranged from rural locations with dispersed residents to high-density urban populations. The seven IMD strands were income, employment, education, health (including disability), crime, barriers to housing and services, and living environment.

Deprivation varied from widespread to hotspots. Many areas had several types of deprivation and were clearly in most need of urgent action. For example, income, employment and health were worse in Blackpool (again), Liverpool, Knowsley and Middlesborough, with neighbourhoods in the last two having the worst education scores.

While those were at the extreme, many other neighbourhoods had multiple deprivation too:

- around 6-in-10 were near lowest scores for at least four types of deprivation;
- around 3-in-10 for at least five;
- and 137 for at least six.

It was obvious where the most help and change was needed. Low income affected over 4-in-10 people and over half the children in the worse areas (2019).

Worse still for PLUs, those living in those more deprived neighbourhoods were more likely to be ‘limited a lot’ by their health conditions. Deprivation and poverty seemed linked to more PLUs, with more limitations and at a younger age. (More on this in Chapter 4.)

So what?

Where you live and how well you did at school can be markers for life expectancy, for being a PLUs-in-waiting, for the severity of that life-changing condition and for life expectancy itself. The odds can be stacked from birth.

CHAPTER 3.

What we do.

Like most PLUs, I too got my disability during my working life but was luckier than many. After various jobs in the Royal Navy, I'd reached the dizzying heights of Lieutenant Commander and become the first woman barrister. I was juggling paperwork, running the Navy's largest 'magistrates court' and strutting my stuff at courts-martial at HMS NELSON, the large shore establishment in Portsmouth. Not the best time for my eyesight to start failing.

I kept going, with increasingly large fonts, and moved to become the Staff Legal Adviser to Flag Officer Plymouth but was 'sick-on-shore' within months. Nearly a year later, blind in one eye and devastated by enormous steroid doses, I squeezed back into uniform. Still able to drive, sporting a monocle, I returned to work on the staff of Flag Officer Surface Flotillas back in Portsmouth.

It didn't take long for the left eye to fail too, and driving was impossible. But, thanks to fabulous support and screen magnification, I was still working, was promoted again and did two more jobs.

The Armed Forces aren't covered by the law when it comes to disability employment, but they'd made the workplace adjustments which meant I could carry on. Naval colleagues, with some exceptions, were hugely supportive despite our culture of 'fit young people'. I must have seemed very strange: probably the first officer wearing uniform and using a white cane for very many decades. But there was no chance of further promotion and medical discharge as a war pensioner followed.

The Royal Navy gave me a precious gift: proof that blindness doesn't destroy either brain or abilities. I had the confident determination to create a whole new career rather than risk my income, mortgage and home.

The law.

The Equality Act 2010 places legal duties on (most) employers. They should make 'reasonable adjustments' when they could know about PLUs on the payroll, should usually avoid health questions when recruiting, and avoid sacking someone because of their health problems. ACAS provides advice to both employers and workers, while Employment Tribunals will decide discrimination claims. Everyone needs to know their rights and responsibilities.

Work prospects.

Most people leave education and move into work based on their qualifications and skills. But we already know that many PLUs-in-waiting didn't do so well at school so may have had more limited choices.

Less school success may be why many PLUs were in lower or middle level jobs in 2021. More were in elementary occupations (such as labourers, cleaners, postal workers) and in middle level jobs (such as administrative and secretarial, caring, leisure and other service roles, sales and customer service).

A positive interpretation is that these employers made the workplace adjustments for their PLUs staff. But, more negatively, some of these jobs may be steps on the journey to life-changing conditions.

> *Recurrent back pain meant that Stephen was unable to work for many years. As he explained: "I was moving heavy bags of sugar, so it wasn't easy to use all the right lifting methods. Over the last 13 years, I have tried to do different sorts of work because it's disheartening feeling that you are not contributing. It's difficult to find an employer who is flexible enough to understand that I may need time off work."*

PLUs were less likely than others to be in skilled trades or working as process, plant, and machine operatives perhaps because they didn't get those jobs in the first place, had difficulty with any adjustments once their health conditions arose or, like others, were just too stubborn to acknowledge the situation.

Steve and Rob are in their early 60s and have been grappling with extreme physical damage for years. Expert joiner Steve's knee injuries finally forced him to give up the tools and use his skills as a self-employed computer-assisted designer. Despite similar extreme knee problems, Rob still fixes cookers (mine twice) to pay off the mortgage. They've been lucky to keep going but, like many others, really need the joint replacements while they can still work, before more injury and while they've got the best chance of recovery.

Of course, some PLUs and those in-waiting get more qualifications or work hard and move into higher level jobs. But fewer PLUs than others were managers, directors, senior officials or in professional, associate or technical occupations (2021). Much may depend on the right opportunities and adjustments. But clearly, simply having a health condition doesn't have to limit ambition or ability. Climbing the greasy pole may make those adjustments easier to get or, like one very senior civil servant PLUs, to keep that condition utterly secret.

Work gaps.

Education finishes, work starts, and life carries on with all the usual ups and downs. Some take short breaks from work to study, to look after the family, for a health problem or even early retirement. Whatever the reason for those gaps, the problems arise if the breaks carry on, which was the revolving door for about two-thirds of those ending up long-term workless PLUs (2021/22).

Keep working.

Becoming workless certainly isn't inevitable. Around half PLUs carry on compared with around 8-in-10 of others. But the health condition or impairment type seems to reduce the chances of keeping that job to:

- 3-in-10 of those with some, often lifelong, conditions such as severe/specific learning disabilities, autism, mental illnesses, or other nervous disorders;
- 4-in-10 of those with sight problems (like me), with progressive illnesses or epilepsy.

About half of those have many different conditions (heart, blood pressure or blood circulation problems, speech impediment, depression, bad nerves, anxiety), and/or physical disabilities (back or neck, legs or feet, arms or hands, chest, breathing, asthma, bronchitis, diabetes). Over 6-in-10 of those have hearing, stomach, liver, kidney, digestive problems, and 7-in-10 of those have severe disfigurement, skin conditions, allergies.

More successful health treatment and workplace adjustments could have improved many of these worker scores. For example:

> *Screen-reader software means I can write this book, and screen magnification was the answer in earlier days. Is there really any good reason other visually impaired people should face such problems in getting and keeping a job?*

Locked up or out?

For some PLUs, there are worse things than just being out of work. Often after petty crimes, about half of prisoners had some form of neurodiversity or mental health condition. Ideally, the criminal justice system isn't the answer.

So what?

Less education success often means lower/ middle level jobs for PLUs-in-waiting. Health conditions may start to show and short work breaks risk being the first step to job loss. But, good news, around half of PLUs manage to keep working (though different conditions have different chances). Better workplace adjustments might improve the odds.

CHAPTER 4.

Poverty.

Gentle reader, you may scoff that I don't know about real poverty. You'd be right nowadays, but that's not always been the case. In younger days, our newly single mother was supporting five children on her nursing pay. Times were tight and we relied on free school meals, had ice inside the bedroom windows in winter, and the weekly orange was a treat. Yes, it was many decades ago and I managed to progress, but still bear the marks.

This little diagram captures some of my thinking from very early days in the disability field about the links between poverty, low education, unemployment and PLUs.

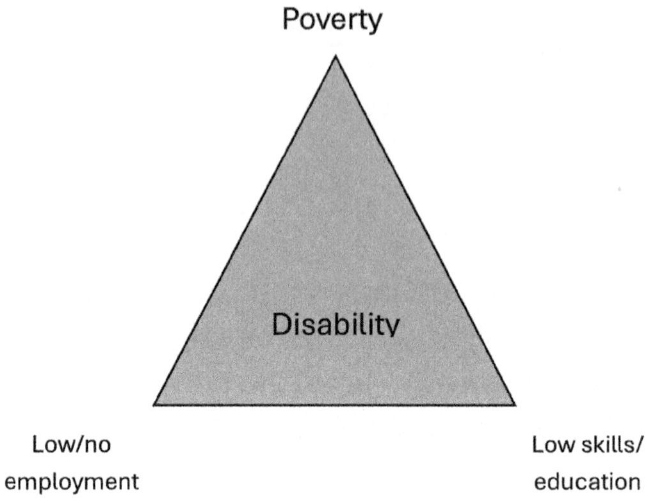

Which comes first? It doesn't matter when it's a vicious triangle.

People.

Life just isn't fair. We've seen half the nation's wealth held by just 1-in-10 and, at the other end of the slippery slope, nearly another 1-in-10 (nearly six million real people and, particularly, PLUs) living in poverty (Institute for Public Policy Research (IPPR) 2024, JRF 2024). The difference between being rich and poor has got wider. At one end, lots of families have become better off over the last ten years but, at the other, absolute poverty reached a 40-year peak (JRF, 2022-23).

- Add one or more PLUs to a family for really bleak prospects. That's a third of all families (about 3 million) with one PLUs.
- It can be even worse for about half those families with more than one PLUs.
- Not even Carer's Allowance levelled out the poverty for many. That family member had to give care for at least 35 hours each week for the allowance of around £80. They could also top up with paid work, but no more than about 12 hours on minimum wage: rather less than £5 per hour for all those 47 hours. When money is tight, every pound counts.

But not even the possible cushion of family care, joint income, shared costs was possible for many PLUs who were more likely to be single and so have even less money: around £3K less each year (RF). Most of those single PLUs were men. They were twice as likely as others to be poor when they relied on benefits rather than working. No wonder they had higher risk of suicide too.

Overall, many people from poor backgrounds became PLUs, which made them even poorer. They had to cope with extra costs, less or no work, relied on benefits and often no partner, or one who couldn't work because of their caring role. In turn, dire consequences for the wider economy: less people working and improving productivity; fewer earning and paying taxes; more relying on benefits. And, often, that poverty passing on to future generations.

Place.

Poverty isn't evenly spread. Some areas have got richer, and others poorer. The England north/south divide is typical: wider and deeper, with the north-east poorest.

We already know that poverty affects success at school, regardless of disability. Pupils on free school meals were *"twice as likely to be absent than others"* (Education Policy Institute – EPI, 2025). Poor 16-year-olds could be nearly two academic years behind the rich kids when they were all taking their vital GCSEs. Having no or low exam grades was probably one reason for the recent peak in young people who weren't in work, studying or training, with increased risk of becoming PLUs, and decades earlier than others.

- Strikingly, the 1-in-4 level of Blackpool residents who were PLUs in their early 40s was only matched by those in richer, leafy Windsor and Maidenhead when they hit their early 70s.

Imagine Blackpool: children seeing their parents with life-changing conditions, struggling or failing to work, family income suffering, and those children perhaps doing less well at school too. No wonder the cycle continues.

Life prospects.

Poverty doesn't just breed disability but early death too. Causes seem to include heart attacks and strokes linked to the low-quality processed food on which more poor families rely (British Heart Foundation – BHF, 2023), and over 30,000 poverty-linked UK cancer cases each year (Cancer Research UK – CRUK). Earlier deaths seem the inevitable result:

- Over a million poorer people died younger compared with those living in the richest areas (2011-19).
- 1-in-10 of those early deaths were linked to the 2010 austerity measures (University College London – UCL).

Poverty for PLUs may be wholly outside our control. Problems can start from where we were born and our parents' health and income, through school success (or not), and work chances to the prospect of earlier disability and death.

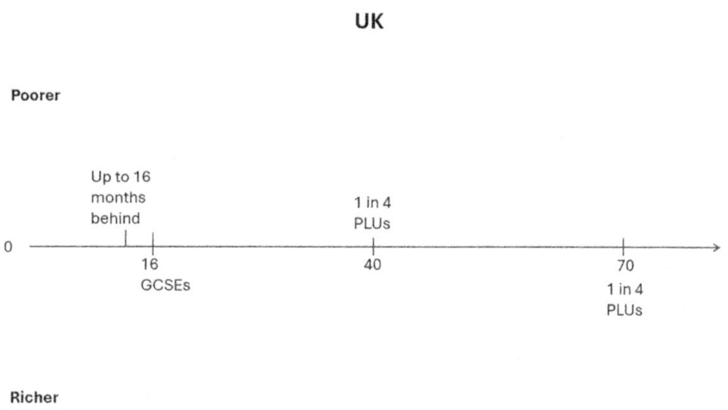

Below the breadline?

Relying on benefits increases the risk of poverty. It's simple: those benefits haven't matched inflation for over a decade and their value was 'frozen' between 2016-20.

> *"The level of benefits available is frequently not sufficient to enable recipients to escape poverty. Indeed, the basic rate of Universal Credit is even below destitution thresholds"* (JRF, 2022).

The bumpy 17 years of rolling out Universal Credit should complete in 2030. The original idea to combine six benefits into one social security payment and "smooth the financial transition from unemployment to work" sounded good but has been dogged by delays, technical issues, IT systems and increased costs. More importantly, the policy may have ignored the reality of claimants' lives.

Imagine the scenario: your last employer wouldn't keep you on because of your health problem and you couldn't get another job. Benefits were the only answer but wasn't a king's ransom. At the start, without any savings, you needed a loan from Department for Work and Pensions (DWP) to cover the weeks before your first payment. Paying it back was painful. Meanwhile, higher bills have made money even tighter. Something has to give, so food and energy costs are the only areas you can 'control'. No wonder that all the stress, poor diet and being regularly cold makes your health worse. Not a lifestyle choice for anyone.

Cutting, freezing or limiting eligibility for disability benefits may seem attractive cost-cutting options for governments, but there is limited evidence that such produce less benefit demand/more PLUs working. Simply putting pressure on PLUs who have least choice, power or agency when trying to work is never likely to be truly successful or worth the political and public backlash. Each of the essential components need action: improvements to the benefits system and how it operates for claimants; effective health and work help for PLUs; changed attitudes and behaviour across all employers who hold the keys to whether PLUs work.

Work as a route out of poverty.

About half working-age PLUs aren't working and numbers have crept up over recent years. We know that those work chances can be limited by our qualifications and the nature of our disabilities. Even when PLUs do work, those with low pay/few hours still need supplementing. But, good news, apparently around a million PLUs would still work if we could. (Some ideas about getting back to work in Chapter 15.)

Poverty can be lifelong.

With half PLUs unable to work and others only able to manage limited hours, retirement can be bleak when surviving on State pensions. Of the working PLUs, more were likely to be self-employed than others but may have put little aside in private pensions.

Another former Wren, Carol, went on to get her degree and worked in the rural housing charity sector. In her early 50s, angina was complicated by rheumatoid arthritis and a lifelong weak immune system. Carol's boss made changes so she could get back to work: an office that avoided stairs and fewer work hours. But less hours meant less 'final salary' private pension that also reduced her state pension. Thank goodness that Navy background helps her keep going.

So what?

Poverty is yet another marker for future PLUs and worklessness. Disadvantaged, deprived communities can be on a downward spiral.

CHAPTER 5.

Getting the treatment we need.

All of us suffer life's wear-and-tear, and most are determined to keep going. But with constant pressures on the NHS, delays and difficulties, it's become more of a challenge and conditions can get worse. While the health system seems busier, productivity may lag behind. Add poor buildings, creaking IT systems, layers of management and staff distracted from their caring vocation for more problems.

In the old Navy days, we were discouraged from registering with a civilian GP as the military wanted control. For me, the HMS NELSON sickbay tried to manage my worsening eye condition before handing over to the uniformed ophthalmologists at (then) Royal Naval Hospital Haslar in Gosport. Terrifying injections into the socket of my right eye didn't work (did I mention that I've been needle-phobic since childhood?).

Ultimately treated by a specialist clinic at the renowned Moorfields eye hospital in London, their solution was massive amounts of steroids and other medication. Within weeks, I was virtually immobile as my body swelled up like the Michelin man. In my mid-30s, it felt odd to rely on my mother, but her nursing skills probably saved me. Returning from the funeral of my nephew, Harry, she found me fighting to breathe while liver and kidneys were on the blink. Easy choice: give up the eye or die.

Poorer outcomes for the poor.

Poverty is closely linked to some conditions such as respiratory and heart diseases, obesity and anxiety. Yet, compared with people who were 'very comfortable', nearly double those 'really struggling' had problems getting GP and dental appointments, and even worse when trying to get mental healthcare and 'feeling listened to' (Healthwatch). Even simple routine screening had lower take-up amongst those scraping by. Negotiating through the health system can be trickier for those who often did less well at school, further increasing their chances of becoming PLUs and decades younger.

A 'universal' health system sounds great in principle, but may not match the different realities of our lives.

Accessibility (in the broadest sense).

Making contact.

Easy contact with the surgery is vital when, for example, more older working age people with two or more conditions mainly depend on their GPs for treatment (LCP). Learning you are in double digits in the phone queue is bad enough. It's worse, when finally getting through, to hear that it's impossible to make an appointment for weeks and then there'll be a competition for the slots. Madness! If AI can work for customer services, perhaps it could work for surgeries too.

Second-class.

Years ago, the then Chief Medical Officer wrote that PLUs with sight and hearing disabilities had more risk of other serious medical conditions. My suggestion of better, disability-friendly communications got a dusty response. However, the NHS Accessible Information Standard (AIS) was introduced in 2016 but never really cut the mustard. Now, years after the Equality Act 2010, the health sector still doesn't comply with the law.

> *In 2025, there was a very distressed husband having to read me the results of a recent health check. Despite having asked them twice for accessible feedback, they'd simply ignored me and sent the standard printed letter.*
>
> *The same often applies to various screening and vaccine offers. Even if you can read the bowel cancer letter, close your eyes and imagine how to capture that stool sample!*

Digital.

Likewise, the online E-Consult forms can be impossible. Never mind us visually impaired people, but how about the *"10% of adults* [who do] *not use, or have access to, the internet at home"* (the Equality and Human rights Commission – EHRC, 2020). It gets worse. Internet exclusion shot up to 6-in-10 of the over-70s living alone with various conditions. Thankfully, the EHRC has 'advised' GP surgeries about digital inclusion (2025).

Understanding.

Even treatment isn't always made easy. Does anyone writing the letters, leaflets or medication instructions realise that the average reading age of the UK population is that of an 11-year-old?

No choice.

Once again, navigating a flawed system on top of ill health and other life difficulties cuts our chances from the outset. When many with most health needs are excluded, the communications aren't working and aren't legal. No wonder calling 999 or turning up at A&E can seem quicker and simpler.

Humanity versus IT systems.

My consultant ophthalmologist, Carlos, and his team at Moorfields eye hospital back in the 1990s were kind, friendly and considerate. It's easy to forget all of those who did excellent jobs whereas the few disastrous ones stand out. Perhaps those negative experiences at times of vulnerability are seared on the memory.

One trying experience, decades later, involved an encounter with a man who called himself a 'tech', and I still have no idea what that meant. Having installed me in a chair, he asked me to cover one eye and read the chart on the wall. Not even my white cane or medical records gave him a clue. He was very upset when I refused, explaining that, even with both eyes, I couldn't see the wall, let alone the chart. He completely lost his cool and I was instantly marched out to see a doctor. Almost certainly not his fault because, as is so common now, his every step was dictated by his computer 'system', designed for an eye hospital but didn't take blind people into account!

There's a real risk that computers become comfort blankets and barriers between the medics and their patients.

> *Exactly the case during a recent physio session meaning that a phone call would have produced the same result and saved the time and effort of being there. Add insult to injury: the proffered exercise plan wasn't available in an accessible format and, clearly, no one had even thought about it. Hasn't it been the law since 2010?*

Broken NHS means more PLUs.

> *Darren had to stop working in 2009 due to a long-term back condition and said, "I'd worked for many of the main dealerships, supervising and managing teams of technicians. So, when I had to stop, it was grim on benefits and money was tight through the long-haul of recovery, treatment and pain management."*

From birth.

Expectant mothers must have been terrified by the Care Quality Commission (CQC) verdict that about two-thirds of maternity units were unsafe (2024). Negligence was causing Mums' birth trauma, brain damage for some babies, and whole families bearing lifetime PLUs consequences.

Young people at risk.

There's been an apparent recent surge in younger PLUs often with mental health or behavioural conditions. Getting SEND assessments and help during school years has become increasingly difficult. Meanwhile, behavioural challenge, substance misuse, self-harm, risk of sexual or other criminal exploitation are known to be often linked to childhood trauma or neglect. Add social media and Covid lockdowns for even more recent toxic risk.

Yet the Supreme Court said the scarcity of places for under-18s with severe mental health conditions or behavioural needs was a 'scandal' (2021). Rather than being placed in suitable secure homes, mental health wards or other regulated therapeutic settings, the courts often could only make 'deprivation of liberty' orders confining those children to unregulated facilities, separated from families and often without treatment.

Although these were probably amongst the most serious cases, they revealed the gap between need and care, spotlighting the long-term personal and economic costs of insufficient early action. Those young people will often have least choice or agency to change the direction of their lives with almost inevitable costs in terms of benefits, care and lost fulfilment.

Other PLUs-in-waiting.

Meanwhile, life for most of us continues but conditions are lurking. Timely health checks and treatment could make all the difference:

- About half of us may get cancer sometime in our lives but, according to *The Lancet*, the odds of survival in the UK were worse than other developed countries such as Canada and Australia (2024). Performance levels were at least a decade behind, older people possibly worse affected and many had slower diagnoses, later and less radio/ chemotherapy.

- Research centred on Birmingham revealed that some 2-in-10 will have sight problems sometime; about half those problems could be treated if caught in time; but around 4-in-10 of those early checks were missed. All-too-familiar life circumstances (living in deprived areas, coming from black and minority ethnic communities, having a learning disability, autism or dementia) made people most likely to miss those checks.
- Likewise, a drop in Type 2 diabetes diagnoses and around half a million people not starting high blood pressure treatment (LCP) represented more missed chances of nipping conditions in the bud.

Root-and-branch change to health checks could offer better health equality for everyone. Conditions multiply. Once PLUs have one life-changing condition, it's easy to get more.

John said, "My life has been dogged by injuries since an attack nearly severed my arm. Then a major cycling accident resulted in several skull fractures, spine and facial damage, only to be followed later by helicopter evacuation from a house fire and near death. Although I've re-trained for alternative careers since, the ongoing consequences meant I couldn't sustain or return to my previous occupations.

As I lost some/all sight, it was automatic to reduce movement to avoid bashing into obstacles and getting injured. (It didn't work when I fell down the stairs.) Less movement quickly became less fitness meaning a constant battle to take enough exercise."

About 4-in-10 visually impaired PLUs are partly/completely cut off from the local community, often have financial difficulties, are less likely than many other PLUs to work, to be independent and self-sufficient. Anxiety and depression aren't difficult to foresee, and other PLUs will have similar tales to tell.

There's more: throw in poor diets that rely on ready-meals, and you have a recipe for disaster. Season with age (many PLUs are 65+ with risk of other conditions) to complete the 'pot-mess' (as we'd say in the Navy).

The medics.

Human too.

Of course, medical professionals are just like everyone else, subject to life and work pressures and wanting to do their best. Often, they may be equal victims of poor systems, inadequate training and too much work pressure. They aren't immune and some will be PLUs too.

> *Talking to someone involved in doctor appraisal, he suggested that, perhaps, 2-in-10 had some level of neurodiversity. It wasn't clear that the profession recognised that this could be a disability needing such legal reasonable adjustments as different methods of record-keeping, accessible IT systems or even support workers. The risk is that competent, capable people may not make the grade with all the lost cost and productivity. For the want of a nail...*

People, not just patients.

Health professionals are key players in how the rest of our lives progress. We can be interesting to them while treatment and interventions are underway. But we may never make the transition from patient to real person so not merit much attention once their box of magic tricks has been exhausted.

> *For visually impaired people, ophthalmologists certify us as sight-impaired/partially sighted or severely sight-impaired/blind. But the reality is that, perhaps, only a quarter of eligible people have been certified. That's a huge number missing out on help ranging from easier benefit entitlement/ tax allowances to practical help from local Social Services. The ophthalmologist probably doesn't realise the huge potential value of their certification and even need reminding by their trainees to use the forms (according to their professional body's guidance)! The cynics amongst us might think that ending payment-by-certificate is the cause; but, perhaps, the medics perceive those certificates as a mark of their failure to cure us (of course, it's not).*

It is always worth checking whether formal recognition of a condition and level of impairment are passports to more help.

Not guinea pigs.

PLUs often have little or no choice but to trust the medics and the government policymakers. But that faith can be shaken. The Infected Blood Enquiry Report (2024) (which seemed a catalogue of errors when it revealed some 30,000 people had been infected with HIV and Hepatitis C), reveals if they weren't PLUs beforehand, due to pre-existing blood and other health conditions, many became so as a direct result of the NHS treatment and their situations made worse by decades of 'institutional defensiveness'.

Amongst the most shocking was the plight of the PLUs children attending Treloar School in Hampshire (where I opened their library years ago). They seem to have been treated as little more than research guinea pigs.

Equality.

> *One of my recent experiences of medication was distinctly grim and I gave up the tablets rather than cope with the side-effects. Perhaps less surprising when I learned that*

most cardio research has been focussed on white men, whereas women and other ethnic groups can have different heart/ body/medication needs. Those ethics committees might think more about equality.

Hopefully, the clamour for a 'duty of candour' will succeed so that all policymakers and others in authority will tell the truth, the whole truth and nothing but the truth at the first time of asking.

Postscript.

'Assisted dying' is on the cards. Choices need to be equal and fair for everyone and not influenced by problems getting health or palliative care. Medics who've been too free with Do Not Resuscitate (DNR) decisions seem risky. Our own GPs have become too remote and weren't even trusted by DWP to make Work Capability Assessments (WCA). Heaven forbid that assisted dying decisions are left to medics or even 'contracted out'.

So what?

Healthcare can improve both our lives and conditions when the medics see us as real people, not just diagnoses/treatments.

CHAPTER 6.

Healthcare hits the fan.

Covid spotlight.

The staff dug deep and deserved their weekly doorstep claps. Contracts for precious PPE were lavishly dispensed. Emergency Nightingale hospitals mushroomed, and vaccines flew into production. The effort, dedication and courage were remarkable, but something had to give.

The health of the population was probably not the best at the start of the pandemic. Smoking, alcohol and junk food had all taken their toll alongside smartphones, social media and algorithms affecting mental health. Echoes of that Fitzroy Report on Boer War recruits.

The virus added its own particular problems such as long-Covid, more mental health risks due to lockdowns, and social isolation.

- There was "*a surge in back and neck problems caused by an increasingly sedentary, obese and ageing population and the rise in remote working*" (ONS).

Changed priorities made routine medicine even more difficult, worse due to 'stay-at-home' edicts and health staff themselves not being immune. Getting an appointment was an increasing challenge if not impossible. E-consults and telephone appointments barely filled the gaps. Most routine treatments and surgery were delayed if not cancelled. Hospital waiting lists shot up. An ONS survey in England suggested that about 2-in-10 over-16-year-olds were waiting for hospital appointments or NHS treatment and that 16-24-year-olds waited longest. Those delayed diagnoses, worsening untreated conditions plus the linked depression or anxiety festered.

PLUs at special risk.

For PLUs, healthcare could already fall short, and the Enquiry report will tell us whether we were treated as well as everyone else. But it seems our chances were worse:

- Double the risk for those with poverty-linked conditions such as obesity, respiratory and heart diseases in England and Scotland.
- Higher risk for those in care or nursing homes.
- Higher risk for those living in over-crowded conditions and/or working in jobs impossible to do from home (particularly key workers).
- Lower vaccination take-up and more difficulty getting healthcare.
- Difficulties with GP appointments meant slow/no initial PLUs diagnosis/treatment. More older working-age people with two or more health conditions mostly relied on GP treatment (LCP).

Even more sinister, it seemed that, unknown and unagreed, DNR flags were added to some of our medical records.

> *I'd heard similar tales decades earlier. A hospitalised university professor with limited mobility discovered DNR on his notes. He was adamant that the value of his life had been judged and found wanting simply due to his wheelchair.*

There was obvious impact on the economy. From around two million workless PLUs in 2019, the numbers had increased by around 800,000 by 2025. More workless PLUs risked more benefit costs, more unfilled job vacancies, less taxes paid and less national productivity and growth.

Peter was one example, happily working as a gardener before the pandemic until a hip was so painful that even his own stubbornness couldn't keep him going. He'd waited years to get the replacement. When it finally happened in 2022, his life had already changed completely. Years unable to work, retired and relocated to a distant county.

Lessons learned.

The UK stood out from many other countries with more deaths and very many more badly affected by the pandemic. More people were reporting mental health conditions, particularly younger ones.

'Over-diagnosis' might be a comforting concept for politicians, cultural warriors and armchair-psychologists; but dismissing clinical evidence backed up by oft-reported real-life experience of violence, misogyny and despair won't resolve the UK's declining health record compared with other countries.

> *Matt was the radio producer/engineer/audio technician (and computer whizz on the side) for an interview I was doing. He described early years of bullying, two suicide attempts and years of not understanding what was going wrong. Eventual autism diagnosis in his early 40s was a revelation. Now he's much happier, able to look back and realise why things were so difficult. Not enough rather than 'over-diagnosis' when there are 2.5 million people in England estimated to have such neurodiversity (2025).*

Whatever the outcomes of the Enquiry and while most people still supported the NHS funding model, confidence had crumbled to 1-in-4. The lowest satisfaction level for 40 years (2024).

Business as usual?

The health service still struggled after the pandemic. Staff shortages, industrial action, headline hospital delays, the scramble for GP appointments shook the system even further and was exacerbated by 'super-user' patients needing high levels of appointments.

> *My first significant experience of the NHS was in autumn 2023. In my mind, with all the Covid-clapping and fondly vague memories of Carry On, Matron, my image was of cheerfully efficient and caring medical folk encased in form-fitting uniforms. Falling down the stairs into a crumpled broken heap opened my eyes to the new reality. 111 phone-triage produced an ambulance. Meanwhile, I'd lumberingly crawled up a chair and tottered to lie prone on a bench. Obviously, such determination was better diagnostically than the excruciating pain: the paramedic decreed no fracture. With lashings of gas and oxygen plus her trainee, I re-climbed those stairs. Her departing treatment advice was over-the-counter painkillers.*

It took more days, another paramedic's stronger medication, more calls and over 20 hours wait for the second ambulance. After five days, I was finally scanned, diagnosed, and admitted to hospital with a vertebra wedge fracture. (I wonder if that original paramedic ever got feedback.)

Another week passed before I had medication I could tolerate. Meanwhile, there were multiple ward changes (one at 0200 to clear the ambulance queue). My memories of the medical, nursing and caring staff are hazy. They certainly did their jobs, were kind and caring when there was time, and supported my recovery. Like nearly everywhere in life, they seemed to spend much time in front of their screens and hadn't any experience of blind patients.

Once deemed fit for discharge, escape home took another week. The hospital bed had been delivered to home but the forgotten mattress came days later! Months in bed, brain medication-befuddled, physio to rebuild mobility followed. Such a simple accident, such huge repercussions. Many others, younger and older, PLUs or not, face such challenges every day.

But the next 'emergency' admission in 2025 went far better. Ambulance, admission, tests, scans, x-rays. Overnight in a recliner being closely monitored by the nursing station. Ward admission (delightful military staff), consultant and discharge within 24 hours – perfect.

So what?

Covid was our wake-up call and showed what is possible (albeit narrowly focussed). Better leadership, management, delivery and results are all possible with the right will and urgency. More involvement of the most vulnerable, most at risk in everyday health delivery and emergency planning could benefit everyone. Fingers crossed...

CHAPTER 7.

Patient tips.

There are lots more, but here are some starters for 10.

Take control.

> *Simon said, "Do not understate our role in our own recovery. Doctors can only do so much; the vast majority is down to us."*

It can be too easy to accept that the medics know best and be a passive patient. We can get better results and avoid potential disasters if we are active partners in our healthcare. Understanding treatment is central to taking part, taking the medication and getting the best outcome possible.

Asking the medics for the treatment plan, the milestones and end result focusses everyone's minds.

During the recent home-recovery, the morning and evening carers were almost all superb in our joint effort. We shared goals and achieved them, even timing showers to score every minute of improvement. Working together meant we could end the care earlier and before means-testing/ funding kicked in.

Knowing what's happening helps focus motivation and determination.

Angela, the physio, explained that patients with other health conditions often worked the hardest, made the most progress and came out best. Thumbs up to PLUs: we may succeed where others don't.

Self-advocacy.

Not being afraid to speak up and have our voices heard and listened to helps make us equal partners in whatever is going on. It's not about whinging or complaining but providing the evidence that the medics need to get their part right. Prepare the questions before the appointment or visit rather than remember it too late.

While I was taking those very high steroid doses in the 1990s, a trainee ophthalmologist decided he'd slash the dose. Thankfully, Carlos, the fellow in charge, was on the ball and listened to my objections. We both knew that the altered dose could have done massive damage.

Decades later, Steve had rehearsed saying clearly that he couldn't tolerate the routine pain medication dished out after manipulation of his knee replacement. He'd collapsed dangerously near the very top of the stairs after a previous dose. Yet, as he recovered from the sedation, the nurse still pressed those pills on him having ignored his medical notes. Thankfully, he had the words and grit to stand firm.

But it's easy to not speak strongly enough as I've done (twice).

During the recent hospitalisation, one low point was the sit-in the-chair episode. They discounted my obviously weak opposition to '30 minutes out of bed in the chair' I'd not sufficiently explained was too low and too small. Two hours later, it took four physiotherapists plus two heavy-duty pieces of equipment to lever me out: forgotten, blind, in pain, befuddled with medication and only partly dressed. They didn't even bother with my patient input to the formal incident report.

The final misery was the porter who'd magically acquired medical expertise. She abandoned the bed transporting me to the discharge unit. Instead, she decided that I could 'walk'. Imagine: barely mobile, in considerable pain, highly medicated, blind, relying on a Zimmer frame to support and find the seemingly endless way. Bullied or what?

Far more positively, on another ward, one patient constantly, day and night, begged "Please help me." There seemed no way to ease her distress but one of the staff patiently sat with her, offering some vital human comfort.

Speaking up is always worthwhile and, ideally, being polite, positive and considerate. Even if we fail at the time, there's always the lure of evidence for the complaint process.

Show them the way.

Although they deal with every one of us PLUs, medics don't seem to get any training on basic disability stuff.

I can't count the number of times I've given the 'basic 1-minute-guiding' session on the hoof as someone has tried to push, pull or steer me around a hospital or similar. "Lie down on the bench" is rarely accompanied by any indication as to which is the head-end. I often had to make sure that medication or water was in the right place on the bedside table where I could find it rather than knocking it off.

There are lots of PLUs about and we can show everyone what works best.

Courage.

Many PLUs show enormous fortitude and determination during the difficult treatments to stop or slow their life-changing conditions. Being brave isn't easy and tears don't matter if you can be resolute and get through often awful treatment.

Sally said, "I wonder how many people coping with a disability are also trying to manage ongoing, invasive and deeply unpleasant treatment. It's the biggest burden I bear, along with the deterioration in sight. Having injections into one's eye (eventually eyes) gets no easier. In fact, it gets worse as the eye seriously does not like being injected on a regular basis (anything between four and eight weeks apart) and, as I know all too well, causes further sight problems. Glaucoma and cataracts being almost the norm. You gain some but lose some as with all treatments."

Perhaps this is a side of PLUs that many don't see or choose to ignore. If policymakers, the media, employers and others realised the massive grit it can take simply to carry on, they might be a bit more compassionate and understanding.

Simple solutions.

Less reliance on badly designed systems, better management and legal compliance, more scope for medics to fulfil their vocations, a smidgeon of respect and better understanding of PLUs rather than just medical conditions could all make the difference we need.

But there's more. An obvious answer would be for the NHS to employ as many PLUs as possible, in every and any role, top to bottom. Attitudes and behaviours would change, systems might meet our needs, there'd be less staff turnover, better outcomes all round. Even more important, when every PLUs in the country is in contact with the NHS at some stage, imagine how they too will change their perceptions, hopes and aspirations when dealing with a fellow-PLUs.

So what?

Rather than leaving PLUs on the healthcare backfoot, learning from us would benefit everyone.

CHAPTER 8.

Strategic change.

Shorter, sicker lives.

Big picture.

Amongst the members of the Organisation for Economic Cooperation and Development (OECD), the UK fell from seventh position for life expectancy in 1960 to twenty-third by 2020 (IPPR). Worse still, the UK *"has seen a slower rate of growth in healthy life expectancy than comparable nations and has a large proportion of preventable morbidity and mortality within its total 'burden of disease'. The UK has rising rates of death and impairment – including higher prevalence of long-term conditions and greater rates of multimorbidity."* More echoes of that Fitzroy Boer War report.

Economic risks versus benefits.

Ill health risks wealth.

"Poor health harms both individual and national prosperity" (IPPR, 2023). It suggested that poor health meant roughly 300,000 people each year stopped working, stopped earning, stopped paying taxes, stopped spending so much and contributed to nearly a million jobs being unfilled (between 2014-19).

> *"Lost earnings have a significant impact on Gross Domestic Product (GDP). We estimate that long-term-sickness-determined loss of earnings cost the UK economy £43 billion in 2021, equivalent to around two per cent of GDP."*

And that was probably an under-estimate as the IPPR recognised their numbers didn't take account of the sick pay, low productivity and other costs of 'short-term sick' people before they left work. (IPPR "Healthy people prosperous lives", 2023).

Ill health increases costs.

Others had calculated the potential cost of mental illness to the UK: some £300 billion, or twice the entire annual cost of the NHS (Centre for Mental Health, 2022). This seems a massive figure but included costs to individuals, their informal carers, and families, to the economy including lost productivity, sickness absence and lost taxes, to the health and care budget. Yet, the figure may still have been an under-estimate because it didn't include the costs of other associated physical and mental conditions, of mental health amongst prisoners, and the increasing level of need.

Perhaps most worrying was that mental healthcare represented only about one-tenth of NHS spending. If every other tenth of NHS spending reflected similar cost to the national economy, better health and preventative treatment across the board would have top priority.

Bleak future.

We already face the prospect of the post-pandemic workless PLUs bulge. Not great for individuals (benefit-dependency followed by pension poverty) or the broader economy. The UK already compares badly with other countries and can't afford to slip further.

Investment?

For example, new dementia medication is on the horizon. But it seems that the treatment needs to be given early so relies on equally early diagnosis. But the UK lags far behind other G7 countries with fewer PET and MRI scanners plus fewer diagnosis specialists. As an electorate, we may want to decide if adequate NHS funding for this and other medical treatment is in our collective best economic and life interest.

Policy predicaments.

New benefit 'assessments' are in the pipeline and are likely to focus on what PLUs can and can't do. Hopefully, there will still be a need for some diagnostic input alongside realistic assessment of claimants' potential. Most importantly, targets need to be economy-wide rather than focus on those with least choice and least agency for change.

So what?

Cross-departmental, top-to-bottom, strategic changes motivated by more than cutting the benefits bill could mean more happy working PLUs, confident employers and a stronger economy too.

CHAPTER 9.

The D-word.

Do I mean disability or denial?

A bit of both. Some very old data from the government's former Office for Disability Issues suggested that across everyone who came within the legal disability definition, nearly two-thirds didn't apply that label to themselves. About the same proportion had no contact with disability-specific organisations.

Of all the Equality Act 'protected characteristics', disability is probably the least desirable yet applies to around 1-in-4 of us. The largest 'minority'.

> *Running back to work projects in Derbyshire, I learned that appealing to 'disabled people' simply didn't work. Putting 'health conditions' front and foremost was far more acceptable and successful.*

Negative reputation.

The disability word can suggest negative undertones that are echoed and amplified by some media and policymakers who should know better.

> *The United Nations Convention Committee said that "the Information Commissioners Office (ICO) has upheld a complaint against the Department for Work and Pensions (DWP) concerning media reports that appeared to be aimed at 'stirring up hostility' towards disabled people claiming benefits. Additionally, the Independent Press Standards Organisation (IPSO) upheld complaints against The Telegraph for inaccurate and misleading articles about disability benefit entitlements that gave a false impression about eligibility and the generosity of the social security system"* (2024).

Not by choice.

Would anyone choose a disabling condition knowing it changes future life prospects, risks unemployment and poverty, being treated as a second-class citizen, publicly vilified and worse? Every fibre of common sense says, emphatically "No!".

Back in 2000, working on the Keeping in Touch project, most of the Incapacity Benefit claimants contacted chose to describe themselves as 'off sick' rather than 'disabled', even though the majority hadn't worked for over two years. Most talked about illness 'holding them back' rather than disability and some criticised an adviser who'd mentioned the D-word. Testament to their denial or continuing ambition?

Test question.

How many people waiting for their hip or knee replacement think of themselves as being PLUs? Not many. Yet they've probably limited their normal day-to-day activities for a long time already. It's utterly understandable. Very few want to be labelled as anything but 'normal'. Others of us bear more obvious signs such as the wheelchair, white cane, guide dog etc.

I remember my first outing with a cane. In those early days, it was the short 'symbol' version to let others know I didn't see much. (Nowadays, I've graduated to the 'long' one to feel a couple of steps ahead.) It was my first public admission of being a PLUs to my hometown: not very different to holding a placard declaring 'Different, broken, needy, second-class citizen relying on the kindness of others'.

Choice may no longer be an option when the medics can't do more, the employer 'lets us go', and money is running out.

It may have been easier for some in the past when the Census question suggested it was acceptable to have a limiting health condition due to 'old age'. But that went in 2021 along with, perhaps, a million who preferred not to tick the box without the age justification.

Stereotyping.

Blind people are supposed to have guide dogs, white canes and use Braille. I love my red stick, which was chosen specially to match my favourite outfits, and don't have the time to care for a dog. As for Braille, I'm told that a tiny percentage of visually impaired people use it (about 20,000 in the UK). Most lose their sight in older years but, by the time we're in our 50s, our fingers aren't sensitive enough to feel the tiny bumps.

There seems to be a common perception that being a PLUs means our brains have been removed too. Not true.

At a recent conference, there was a company law consultant, a tax specialist, an ex-rugby player and singer, a defence professional, a retired barrister/director and, a couple of retired business people and many more. Yet others still labelled us by our disability rather than seeing the real people we are.

Trumpet blowing.

One organisation I led as a blind person had an annual budget of nearly £250m (and that was back in the early 2000s). Influencing government policy as a Non-Executive Director on the board of HMRC, chairing and working for other government, charity and voluntary bodies, running a business, winning awards and an international prize were just part of the following decades' activities. Navy: eat your heart out!

Policymakers in denial too.

Hats off to the last Census efforts to get better PLUs data. They added mental health conditions to match the law so higher numbers should have been no surprise; but not what the policymakers wanted with mutterings about self-diagnosis, scrounging and more.

Reality.

> *Without any sight at all, some people think that I spend my life 'in the dark', that I'm 'black blind'. Perhaps some have that experience, but my life is constantly bathed in cool early summer sunshine, day and night. Others get distressed by switching off the lights when they leave me in a room. I don't care at all except for saving on the electricity bill.*

> *Others don't see: the phenomenal 3-D (to the millimetre) spatial recall needed to avoid collisions; hearing acute enough to detect gas escaping from the bottle of fizz; sensitivity so heightened as to detect others' imperfect truths; incredible powers of concentration; phenomenal reading speeds. And that's all just every day.*

Humans are wonderfully adaptable to survive but can be amazingly blinkered to others who do so.

Warning.

Blind PLUs are supposed to be the best lie detectors. We can hear how your breathing changes, your vocal cords tighten, your hesitations, pauses and distractions. And it's easy to hone those skills listening to politicians and their spin-doctors! Other PLUs have extra skills too, so don't under-estimate us!

So what?

Labels (especially the negative ones) change attitudes and behaviour.

CHAPTER 10.

Bereavement, grief and worse.

Bereavement curve.

The classic diagram below describes many of life's ups and downs, whether loss of a loved one or loss of an essential part of oneself.

Bereavement curve

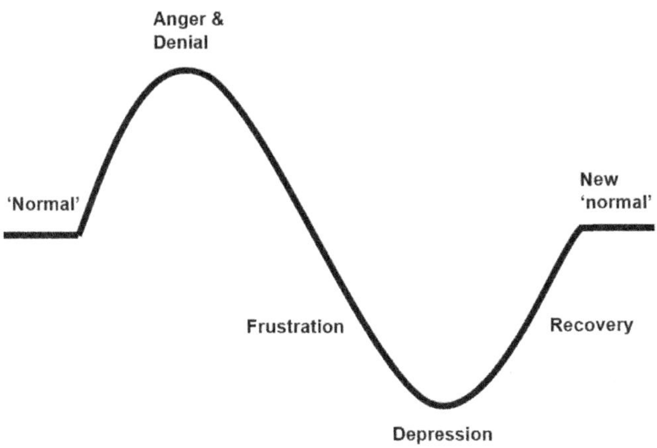

The curve moves from left to right, from 'normal' up to a peak of emotion: anger and denial. The downward curve then drops through frustration into a trough of depression. With luck and the right help, that trough isn't too deep and doesn't last too long before rising up again to the new 'normal'.

Grief.

How fragile is our sense of 'self', who we are and our place in the world? By its very definition, any disability is life-changing. Previously, we probably had most of the right bits in the right places, both bodily and mentally. We had our roles in life, family, friends, work, hope, ambition, happiness, self-image and sense of ourselves.

Now there's a new scenario. For some PLUs, it may have arrived with a crashing shock. For others, a gradual creeping change. Either way, grief, bereavement and despair are perfectly normal.

> *All this kicked in during the early stages of my sight loss. The first impact, imagining*

what was to come and the disastrous consequences were shattering. Mental health support from a Royal Navy psychiatrist helped with memories of past resilience. His confidence regalvanised my own and the fight was on.

But sight loss wasn't the worst of it. The risk to work and income, mortgage and home, loss of independence and ignorance about help and benefits were all critical.

Like a rocket trip to the moon, PLUs need to know how to navigate the system, keep ourselves warm and fed, survive financially and overcome being treated like an 'alien'. Knowing and understanding can be early steps to recovering the 'right mind-set' (Chapter 13) and emerging from that trough of despondence. We need to learn what is still possible within the new 'normal'. After all, we often entered the life-changing maze with the same ignorance and prejudices as everyone else.

Adaptive technology and passenger assistance were my early stepping stones.

But our minds may need still more reassurance that the essential person, within ourselves, remains.

Depression, anxiety and worse.

For many PLUs, the immediate health situation may have eased with rest, recovery and medication, but the mind is still facing an alien future, stuck somewhere, often at home, separated from previous life routines, from interactions with other people, from familiar fulfilling activities and more. Even if we still look and think much the same, some bits are broken. Good professional help can be the answer.

> *The myriad Help To Work providers in Derbyshire realised the risk: additional mental health conditions could quickly result from the isolation caused by other life-changing conditions and unemployment. Once recognised, solutions weren't hard to find. Everyone (partners, community health nurses, clients themselves) worked to link those in need with professionals and self-help groups.*

The American Surgeon-General also described mental and other health consequences, saying:

> *"The highest prevalence for loneliness and isolation among people with poor physical or mental health, disabilities and others." He assessed their additional health risks: "Loneliness and social isolation increase the risk for premature death by 26% and 29% respectively [...] increased risk of disease, including a 29% increased risk of heart disease and a 32% increased risk of stroke [...] increased risk for anxiety, depression and dementia [...] may increase susceptibility to viruses and respiratory illness" (2023).*

A catalogue of miseries and ill health if we don't get out enough. Although these figures come from the USA, it is probable that lonely and socially isolated PLUs in the UK will face similar problems.

Most seriously, PLUs seem to have had three times as much risk of suicide compared with others and worse for middle-aged men.

The "highest rate of suicide was amongst disabled men aged 40 to 50 years [...]. Overall, the rates were lower in women compared to men" (ONS).

We know that life-changing conditions coincide with middle-age amongst those already living in poverty; but men may be less likely to seek help and, anecdotally, both men and women may have similar suicidal thoughts, but men tend to act. However, female PLUs still had a higher suicide rate than other women. For all, PLUs status was probably more significant than any other socio-economic factors. Jobs also seemed important as suicide rates increased among the long-term unemployed or those who'd never worked. Easier said than done for PLUs.

Paul's history is similar to so many people who have worked hard for years until ending up on benefits due to ill health. After nearly 30 years in traffic management, he was a self-employed safety control officer responsible for all the legal rules about motorway contraflows and their thousands of traffic cones.

However, as Paul described: "Twelve-hour shifts working amongst the noise of motorways damaged my hearing. Ear defenders seem the answer but can be even more risky. It was only because I heard the tyre burst that I'm here today, otherwise the out-of-control lorry would have run me down. But I also started having intermittent severe headaches and memory loss so that I was disorientated with mood swings. It was really worrying and scary for all the family. My condition has never been diagnosed after lots of scans, different drugs and treatment.

"Other people couldn't see that I was ill, so they didn't understand because I look as fit as anyone else," he explained. "I ended up on benefits in 2009. I was ashamed of not being able to support my family as the illness had stripped away everything."

Yet another long-term PLUs said: "I'm not a man anymore because I can't provide for my family."

Wider costs.

The Surgeon-General also considered the financial consequences:

> *"Billions of dollars for additional medical and economic costs caused by poor social connections on top of the consequences for individuals and their communities." He described those connections as "important as food, water and shelter [...] creating a more 'critical public health concern' than smoking, diabetes or obesity."*

Closer to home, without being over-dramatic, there may be community-wide trauma that creates long-term ill health and disability.

> *Over ten years running projects in Derbyshire focused on the enduring pockets of poor health, disability and unemployment. Locations with mining backgrounds, rather optimistically described as having 'services and industrial legacy', can have the greatest need in relation to health, disability and unpaid care (ONS). Long after the strike traumas and pit closures, these remain areas of greatest health inequality with*

many unable to work due to their sickness or unpaid caring responsibilities. A double whammy of lost earnings that drives their poverty, possibly reinforcing trauma and local despair.

Carrying on.

Life goes on and we have to learn ways of coping with the new 'normal' amidst huge uncertainty. But other people's reactions have impact too. Kindness is good but not if smothering. Being treated like a child makes us powerless. Others are feeling their way, and we need to help them understand. Anger is easy, but gentle while firm may work better. Some simply run a mile in case it's catching. Forget them. (More about attitudes in Chapter 12.)

Being able to keep working in the Navy as my sight disappeared probably saved me. Constantly in touch with others, busy and productive, I proved to myself that I was still capable.

Getting lost in the bushes wasn't a failure but gave the security guards a chance to rescue me. I'd rebuilt the confidence to keep doing pottery, swimming, volunteering, giving a wild millennium party and designing a new conservatory. All down to other people's trust and faith.

Families, friends, colleagues and even the odd professional play vital roles: supportive but not over-protective; patient while we rant about the unfairness; laughing with us; still valuing us. But it doesn't take much to damage fragile confidence.

The benefit sanction system 'presumption of guilt' approach risked increasing fear and anxiety for PLUs (and others) (Public Law Project – PLP, 2022).

Still hope.

David said, "From a three-year downward spiral of depression and overdoses, I decided that I couldn't get any lower but had to bounce back. I wanted to be the person I used to be. Depression is an illness, but it can be beaten with determination, support from friends and family and the right treatment. Now I can work and I've got a purpose in life. It's good to know there's a light at the end of the tunnel for people with depression and other conditions."

So what?

PLUs often have psychological and mental health consequences on top of our life-changing conditions.

CHAPTER 11.

Getting the help we need.

Hearts and minds.

Don't be shy.

There's a lot of help out there, but finding it through the different systems can be tricky when coping with health treatment, pain and misery. Information isn't always easy to get or understand, worse for many put off by 'officialese'. Add the daunting life-changing prospect of the D-word label and, insult to injury, having to seem grateful too!

Loughborough University suggested that a quarter of registered visually impaired PLUs were dipping out (2024). Reasons included the stigma of claiming, struggles with face-to-face interviews plus inaccessible information and claim processes. Other familiar personal factors played their part in low take-up too: age;

fewer 16-44-year-olds; minority ethnic groups; men; those in low-income households.

Avoidance might seem easier but asking is about courage, determination and motivation. Those guarding the purse strings shouldn't put us off.

Family and friends can be indispensable while there are myriad government, voluntary and condition-specific charities out there, both nationally and locally. Using them all makes sense in getting the best answers and information. Having an expert on side can take the pressure off and, after all, it's what they're there for! Being well-informed helps in tackling officialdom at every level.

> *Years ago, I was applying for Disability Living Allowance (DLA). At that time, there was a booklet of over 50 pages asking for all the details of my health and its consequences. Not easy with sight loss. Thank goodness for a local charity that could steer me through the process, fill in the paperwork and help me succeed. More recently, Kimberley said, "It's still no easier. It's horrendous, which is why I (and others no doubt) gave up!"*

Rest assured, the following doesn't attempt to cover everything but is just an overview.

Independence.

Life-changing doesn't always have to be negative but can offer good points, new experiences, different successes. Searching out the right advice, new ideas, practical solutions can bring fresh independence.

The huge heavy adult electric trike meant I could still get around once driving was impossible. I loved that trike. I could manage the couple of miles to the shops and be independent. But keeping the battery charged was more of a challenge. Often, pedalling valiantly up the long hill home, pedestrians would cheerfully greet me as they strolled past. But that simple freedom evaporated when I could no longer see the kerb.

A Blind Veterans UK visit to Paris decades ago proved to me that solo travel needn't be a problem. Good planning and maximum use of Passenger Assistance meant going all over the world and UK for work and fun for decades.

Family and friends.

Familiar support circles are often the first port of call, but not everyone is willing or able. Some Trojans will do sterling jobs, sustain relationships, offer the helping hand and even become that invaluable 'informal carer'. Others simply stop calling.

One relative complained, "Don't do it like that. It makes you look blind." Of course I was, but he still couldn't accept it. Another simply refused to move as I struggled to get through a tight corner.

For those who disappear, won't help or worse, it's their problem so let them go. There are more important people.

The girls' shopping trips, the theatre and dinner outings, flower arranging, pottery and pewter-smithing sessions all stay possible because of them. The important people strike the delicate balance between letting me get on with life and stepping in if needed.

New friends are a true bonus. Some are in similar situations and have great tips to share. Others aren't daunted and accept PLUs on our own terms.

Getting information.

The law says that any organisation (government, business or voluntary) providing services to the public has an anticipatory duty to make reasonable adjustments for PLUs. That can mean making information and services accessible (in the widest sense). And anticipatory means they have to get it as right as possible without us having to ask. These days, many of those organisations seem to think that online information fits the bill, but forget that many can't use the internet: it's not accessible for some and 'officialese' is meaningless for many. There are international website accessibility standards that provide a starting point. However, it still takes skill, determination and time to find out what we need to know.

Back in the 1990s, I was struggling to discover help for when I left the Navy. I wrote to DWP suggesting a simple directory that would help. There wasn't any interest then but, a decade or so later, I created the 'Help To Work' catalogue of some 50 organisations operating in part of Derbyshire: short, to the point, and aimed at PLUs wanting to get help. It was online, but at least a start.

Getting help from someone else can still be invaluable and a second opinion never hurts. Everyone (including those working in government departments, the NHS, the business and voluntary sectors, and PLUs) needs to know what the Equality Act allows and doesn't. After all, 1-in-4 of us may be fighting for our rights at some time.

Evidence helps.

Collecting the medical letters, the medication details, the diary of what's happened and what's been impossible is worthwhile. Lots of decisions use medical 'evidence', which is good at labelling conditions but not always for measuring what PLUs can and can't do. Relying on the medics too much isn't best use of their time nor best for PLUs either.

Instead, we are the experts on how our lives have changed and can describe everyday reality (but avoid misleading 'best-case scenarios'). Our information helps the decision-makers across those myriad organisations understand our individual circumstances.

> *For one critical assessment, I turned up with a graph showing how my failing sight linked to specific incidents! Probably rather OTT (over the top) but it worked.*

If we don't agree with their assessment, we've got the evidence to back up our case and, again, having an expert on our side can make a dispute or appeal easier.

> *Ex-Navy pal Chris has kept his diary of medical conditions for over 15 years, capturing brief details of his symptoms, test results, diagnosis, treatments and their impact, with dates of all the different contacts with various parts of the NHS. He explained, "The reason for the diary is that I got fed up with being asked, have you*

> *had this treatment or that treatment, or when did you have radiotherapy, and when was the last time you had scans, MRI, PET, ultrasound etc. It also records some of the frustrations in dealing with the admin side of healthcare. So, I just carry the diary with me every time I see a doctor or healthcare worker and hand it to them. The last time I used it was when I had a PET scan recently, which discovered cancer in the throat. I handed the list to the doctor because they had given me a form to fill in which had a box about a centimetre deep which said: 'State previous medical history'. After the scan, he handed the diary back to me and said, 'Thank you. I have read all of this', followed by a pause, then, 'Amazing, you look so well'."*

If it helps, my brother Peter's 'What just happened' app (free on App Store) might be useful.

Practical help.

Some PLUs need regular help for life and/or work, often paid. It can mean juggling funding from personal money, government and charities to pay the bills. Even if such help is affordable, working through the regulations can be difficult. Recently, the rigid rules for Carer's Allowance have been under the microscope as they limit the carer to not much more than slave labour.

Likewise, employment 'status' of other paid helpers needs attention. PLUs may be unable or unwilling to take on an employer's legal and pension responsibilities for paid help, but 'self-employment' only stands up if meeting HMRC's definition. Agency help can seem easier but more expensive.

Extra everyday help.

> *A simple trip to the doctor or dentist means taxi fares, upgrading vital screen-reader software costs a fortune, help at home has kept me clean and safe for decades, and there's so much more... but it isn't free!*

In the old days before 2013, PLUs had DLA and Attendance Allowance (AA) to help offset our additional costs of having a life-changing condition. Now Personal Independence

Payments (PIP) is taking their place for many. Importantly, none of these benefits has anything to do with whether PLUs are working or not; they are not 'means-tested'.

Room for improvement.

It is very easy for the media, public figures and closer contacts to typecast everyone on benefits as 'scroungers' without understanding our real situations. Of course there are fraudulent claims, but there's official error too. Rather than just counting the financial costs, knowing that nearly 7-in-10 PIP appeals succeed shows the scale of those mistakes. Nevertheless, suspicion can be difficult to counter or survive.

PLUs may have very similar attitudes about claiming. Another piece of precious self-identity is torn away: no longer fit and healthy like everyone else; unable to hold down a job; now having to rely on the charity of benefits. Desperation rather than desire may be the driving force. It was estimated that nearly £19b of (all) benefits weren't being claimed each year.

More 'universal' support along the lines of Child Benefit and the Coronavirus Job Retention Scheme could cause less stigma and so have far higher take-up. Combined with a single accessible source of simple information, more standardised eligibility criteria, good advice and help, the support might be more useful for many and cheaper to run.

The way ahead.

DWP is looking again at PIP (2025), how the assessment process works, and using it for unemployment benefits too.

> *There were myriads of different documents and processes for medical discharge from the Navy: certification of blindness, war pension, Social Services help, Disability Living Allowance, Access to Work, Blue Badge, council tax, and doubtless more I've forgotten.*

There's nothing wrong in principle with a single, simple multi-purpose process for every type of help (which also makes work more possible). But any health 'professionals' involved need the right qualifications and experience. Likewise, better processes that reduce suicide rates, official error and delays would be excellent, although relying on Artificial Intelligence runs the risk of further embedding the prejudice and discrimination already obvious from 'sick-note-culture' accusations. While so many appeals succeed, there's obviously too much going wrong with the current systems meaning they're no basis for the future.

Out of work help.

Again, the DWP benefits have changed over the years from Incapacity Benefit (IB) and Employment and Support Allowance (ESA) to progressively become Universal Credit (UC), which takes account of age, single/partner situation, means-tested household income and savings, health assessment and date of claim. And more changes are afoot with the possibility of an adjusted PIP measure replacing the notorious WCA (2025).

Room for improvement.

The reputation of the DWP benefits system has suffered from allegations about the unfairness, distress and poverty it causes. The EHRC started a statutory investigation based on suspicion that DWP hadn't made the adjustments needed by PLUs with mental health conditions during assessments and decisions, causing substantial disadvantage (2024).

More extreme, the National Audit Office said that the 69 claimant suicides between 2014-20 were 'highly unlikely' to have been the true number and that more evidence than just coroners' reports was needed (2020).

Media tales of 'sanction targets', fake job vacancies, 'conditionality', hyper-judgemental assessments, claimant stress (even those suicides), discourtesy and delays topped with high appeal success rates may have varying truth but shape our trust and appetite for more struggle.

Responsibility?

Of course, unemployment due to a health condition begs the question as to why the previous employer didn't make the changes to keep that PLUs in work. More of this in Chapter 16, but perhaps the benefit system shouldn't be used to offset any unlawful behaviour.

In work help.

For those PLUs able to keep or get new jobs, Access to Work funding has been available for many years from DWP to help with the extra costs of adaptive equipment, travel to work and support workers. In reality, the vast majority of workplace adjustments are simple and straightforward, not costing employers or PLUs anything much. ATW should help with the rest, if it is available quickly enough for the job start. But recent reports of delays put those jobs at risk (2025).

The way ahead?

There's an underlying conflict in the benefits approach. On one hand, PLUs have to describe the challenges of life for PIP, ATW and unemployment benefits while, on the other, need to promote our capabilities to employers. Perhaps the current systems can't manage such cognitive dissonance?

There's even been chatter about getting rid of DWP because the ethos developed over years seemed more about penny-pinching and targets than good lives for real people. Perhaps over quarter of the population (including the carers, war pensioners, SEND pupils and more) justify higher political visibility. A centre of excellence led and manned by PLUs, with power and influence, could change policies and behaviour across all levels of government. We already know what needs doing and, rather than the current departmental silos, action based on our actual lives and potential could be revolutionary for the whole economy.

Voluntary sector.

Charities, whether general like Citizens Advice Bureaux (CAB), or condition-specific, also have much to offer, although old data suggested that around two-thirds of PLUs had no contact with the last. They can fill important gaps, provide valuable advice, expertise and practical support, but only if we find them and ask.

Trustees have their own responsibilities and personal liabilities to run sound, lawful organisations that fulfil their purpose (the charitable objects) and use their funds properly.

> *One charity for (rather than of) PLUs with sight loss incurred my wrath. The email asked for my details either using an online form or by phone. The form didn't work with a screen-reader and the phone service asked for the registration number of a car I've never seen, let alone driven or handled its paperwork! The return caller was clearly switched to transmit rather than receive, oblivious to the needs of blind people. I gave it up as a bad job.*

Charities work best when beneficiaries have a voice that's heard, ask the right questions and have ideas to contribute. Potential donors should be looking for a good staff/beneficiary ratio, evidence of resources well-used, needs identified and met, respect rather than condescension, compliance with the Nolan Principles, a set of seven ethical standards for UK public office holders, and the law. However, this isn't always the case.

> *A solicitor concerned with Wills highlighted how donations could be lost amongst staff costs and other activities so it's worth checking the last annual report, calculating expenditure and assessing the charity's value to the beneficiaries before leaving that legacy.*

There's more.

On top of the legal protection at work and elsewhere, some PLUs can get special help during their education years, extra tax allowances from HMRC, war disablement payments from the Ministry of Defence, personal health budgets from the NHS, lower council tax bands, blue parking badges and even free parking, reduced train fares, passenger assistance for trains and planes, lower prices at theatres (and elsewhere), extra help while shopping, special training for life adaptations, equipment to make living easier, special social events and very much more. Just asking is the first step towards a treasure trove!

So what?

Finding the right help can present even more hurdles: accepting the PLUs future; navigating through masses of information; locating the right advice; working through multiple 'systems'. All take their toll.

CHAPTER 12.

Attitudes.

Most people's first reaction to 'disability' is about lifts and ramps. That wildly unrepresentative blue parking badge/sign has a lot to answer for. In contrast, for PLUs, it's other people's attitudes that are often the biggest challenge. I tried to reflect this in the Disability Dynamics (DD) model:

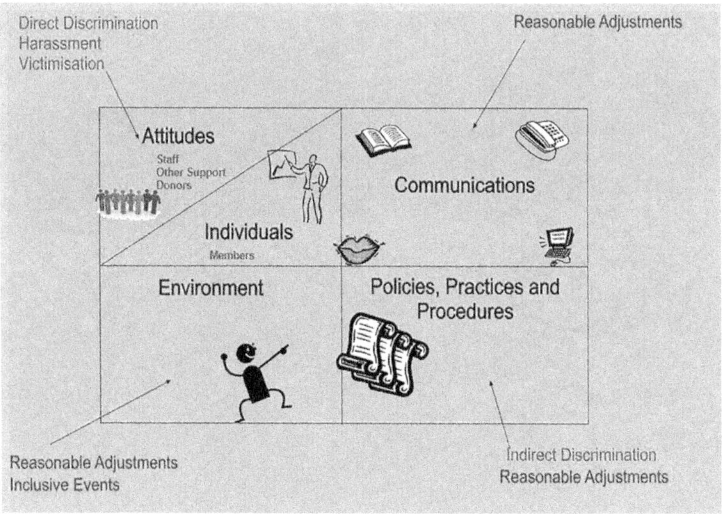

Each quarter links with the relevant bits of the Equality Act covering direct and indirect discrimination plus reasonable adjustments.

The first quarter covers Attitudes. These could be the ideas, beliefs and misconceptions of the employer, the public sector organisation, the service provider, the landlord or anyone else (from top to bottom of their people pyramid) that drives their behaviour and actions. Alongside are us, the PLUs, whether the worker, patient, client, customer, tenant or friend.

I borrowed the 'swingometer' idea to show all those different attitudes:

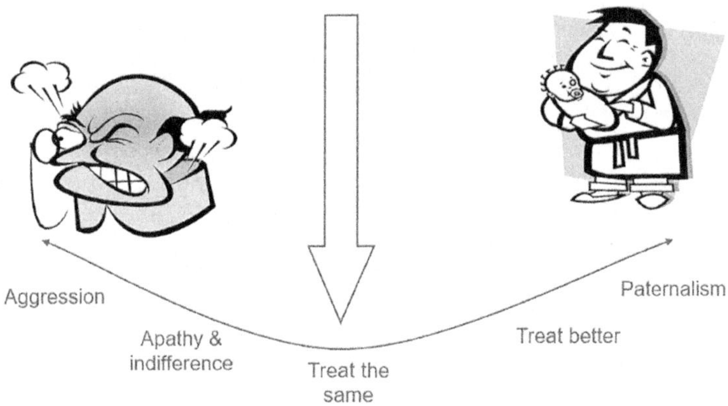

Yes, we really do experience all those negatives! The swingometer lurches between the extremes of paternalism and aggression. Thankfully, the latter is less common, although others assuming we can't make our own decisions is common. Simply ignoring PLUs is frequent. We can see it every day in how the world tries to operate as if we don't really exist.

Imagine having to pacify the abusive woman who totally denied that I was blind when our trolleys clashed. Clearly, she believed the white stick was purely decorative!

> *A TV programme was due to feature a client's award-winning business, but the publicity produced those negatives: his car had already been vandalised; tyres slashed; his visiting adviser's car had a non-repairable puncture. No one could prove anything; but a PLUs getting above himself was obviously fair game for the locals.*

Treating us 'the same' seems obvious, but 'better' is the right answer that takes account of those reasonable adjustments. It's that little bit of extra thought, consideration and planning that gives PLUs the chance of an equal, level playing field. Those changes often cost nothing, or very little when designed in at the start, but can be life changing.

Even so, an organisation, shop, employer or other can have all the adaptive software and equipment, disabled car parking and loos, inclusive policies and equal personnel procedures. But all that effort is wasted if their people don't have positive attitudes to match. And I'm not convinced that online training will do the trick.

> *Having pitched up for a meeting at an organisation's national London headquarters, the receptionist asked me to sign in. He took it as a personal insult when I asked where to sign and where was the pen. Worse, I asked for help to find the lift. His swingometer was distinctly left leaning and you can imagine my feedback to the meeting!*

Risks.

As covered before, government, business and voluntary organisations providing services to the public have responsibilities to anticipate those reasonable adjustments PLUs might need. Making sure that staff attitudes and behaviour are right is worthwhile when a kind word, helping hand, practical solution can defuse situations. The alternative of getting it wrong is a gamble on possible complaints, legal action and losing, perhaps, a quarter of customers. The risk increases for organisations catering for higher levels of PLUs, our families and supporters (such as the NHS, elements of government concerned with jobs, benefits, pensions, care etc) and PLUs charities. Reputational risk of getting attitudes wrong needs attention too when PLUs are so frequently in the news.

Stereotypes (again).

The D-word often conjures up those obvious stock images (wheelchair, guide dogs, Braille and white canes, hearing loops etc) for employers and service providers. In fact, most life-changing conditions are hidden (e.g. cancer, mental ill health, neurodiversity and many more). Perceptions of PLUs' lives can be equally stereotyped (different, quite sad and poor, choosing benefits over work, old). It smacks of denial: strong, fit, successful people like me don't end up like that.

Conflicting ideas.

> *"Cognitive dissonance is a psychological term that describes the discomfort we feel when we hold conflicting beliefs or attitudes, or when our actions don't align with our beliefs. It's like having two pieces of a puzzle that don't fit together, and it creates a kind of mental tension or unease"* (AI interpretation).

Conflicting ideas about who PLUs are and what we can do create just such tension. Common beliefs could be 'work-shy scroungers who irritatingly get the best parking slots', which are at odds with more personal ideas about 'the dear old relative who is shaky on her pins, needs her shopping done, is sad and lonely'. Likewise, PLUs can have similar mismatched ideas: still burning to make a mark in life, but told by everyone we are no longer fit or able.

While none of these are probably wholly true, it isn't comfortable to use one set of ideas, values, words and actions in, say, the workplace or home, when a completely different set applies outside. It can be easy to adopt the 'group-think' of different environments, but having to juggle values and reality just to fit in can breed all sorts of unhappiness, anxiety, embarrassment, sadness, shame, stress, powerlessness, guilt, damaged self-image. Not a happy place to be.

Many times, when I've delivered disability training, some attendees have had that lightbulb moment as they recognised how the 'label' applies to a friend, relative or even themselves. They usually expressed enormous relief having realised that the label is just that, and doesn't cover the full reality and complexity of life, in and out of work.

I suspect that the receptionist (above) couldn't compute the conflicting situation of an obviously disabled person purporting to join a very senior meeting in his headquarters, so discomfort bled into his behaviour.

Avoiding the conflict.

Some will avoid thinking, talking or doing anything to remind themselves (or others) about the clashing ideas. How often are PLUs told we're 'inspirational' or 'exceptional' by someone who wants to avoid the fact that we're just normal. Alternatively, PLUs may avoid a new activity because being risk-adverse has become the norm.

Pretending.

This happens when words and behaviour don't really match one's beliefs but make the situation easier and hides the differences from other people. It's like paying lip service to the equality policy, but knowing that differences **do** matter, and a PLUs job applicant won't make it.

Undermining.

Some will assume ignorance, bias or even dishonesty to undermine the person or event that revealed those mismatched ideas. For example, rubbishing the report about PLUs wanting to work because it doesn't match the idea of 'scroungers'.

Positive unease.

A bit of discomfort can do us good. The AI tool continues:

> *"Our brains strive for consistency, so when there's a mismatch between our beliefs and actions, it triggers this discomfort. Recognising and understanding cognitive dissonance can actually help us make better decisions and align our behaviours with our values."*

A bit of dissonance can be good if it keeps us open-minded to new ideas and willing to change our own. But be wary of denial that limits our worldview to entrenched ideas and narrow self-image.

Changing hearts and minds.

Some ideas that might help PLUs, those who help us, the medics, the bosses and work colleagues etc.

Self-control.

Sometimes it's tough to keep a civil tongue when others' entrenched beliefs result in foolish behaviour: ignoring or abusing PLUs; the superiority of knowing what's good for us. Confrontation can simply reinforce prejudice. (On the other hand, sometimes it helps to vent frustration.)

> *One young man purportedly tasked to guide me at Brussels airport declined to pull my carry-on bag. How could we manage when my own hands were full of a white cane and holding his arm? I drew out a Dictaphone (yes, it was that long ago) and asked him to repeat his refusal. It was as if I'd pulled a gun on him! Worth saving the rough-tough stuff for one-off encounters.*

Exposure.

Even though PLUs are 1-in-4, when so many conditions are hidden and brave faces conceal life's challenges, it's easy for others to pass by without noticing. Training, information, more interactions and more openness from us can help others see we're real people rather than stereotypes.

> *After years delivering disability training, I'm humbly sure that, rather than the outstandingly wonderful content, success was due to the groups' realisation that I was just like them: enthusiastic but fallible; professional but human.*

Self-image stroking.

Most people want to be thought of as caring, compassionate, kind, considerate when dealing with PLUs. Helping them to showcase their positive qualities can strengthen their self-image, encourage them to do more and even develop. Their early steps could be as simple and easy as ensuring breaks during meetings, knowing the location of the disabled loo, providing accessible information, not second-guessing medical evidence. Don't stint on fulsome praise to stroke those egos.

> *If that receptionist had handed over the pen and guided my hand from the start, he'd have had huge gratitude and a big smile.*

Subtle steering.

Often PLUs have to rely on others. Honing our person-power skills can get the best out of them.

> *Those on-the-spot guiding lessons for someone fearful have paid dividends. The physical contact of holding their arm, a couple of minutes explaining the basics, practicing together and I've got a guide for the whole visit and they're much more confident... or terrified of white canes!*

Power-play.

PLUs are often used to being the 'under-dog' but there are lessons to be learned from our canine friends. Without tails to wag, the lightest touch of 'subservient' gratitude, beseeching eyes and nodding head suggest willing compliance. It goes against the grain but, sometimes, a little deference wins the day and soothes others' anxiety.

Bearing witness.

Tasking a nay-sayer to personally collect information and ideas from PLUs is useful. The insights can be shared widely while the celebrated author is unlikely to contradict those findings.

So what?

For PLUs to get a fair chance, everyone needs to realise that we're all the same, that disability isn't a lifestyle choice and that we have least power for change.

CHAPTER 13.

The right mind-set.

Imagine what it's like: told by your doctor that you have a life-changing health condition; biting the demoralising bullet of describing everything you can't do anymore when claiming help towards all the extra costs; your employer tells you there's no place for you if you can't do the job; claiming the long-term sick benefit is dreadful recognition of how life has changed. No wonder PLUs are at such high risk of depression as we foresee the rest of our lives crumbling.

> *A young, ex-veterinary nurse described her need to get back to work although she'd recently lost much of her sight and mobility. She talked about having 'the right mind-set': avoiding depression when life is overwhelmed by medical problems; being stuck at home; being poor and often isolated; when the future is bleak and there aren't any obvious solutions.*

She showed extraordinary resilience. If only employers and policymakers recognised the determination and motivation.

D-word models.

In the past, the 'medical model' was rejected for defining PLUs by our health conditions. The 'social model' was better as it blamed society's failure to make adjustments for causing our disablement. But there's more:

> *Years ago, a PLUs' activist said he wanted to get back to work. We'd done our best to get him ready and even lined up an enthusiastic and willing employer. But he seemed to sabotage the interview. Perhaps he disliked the prospect of becoming a little fish in a big pond, didn't have enough self-confidence, or was wedded to his outcast status.*

I learned that no model of disability survives without including the individual's mind-set in the mix. Hence PLUs feature alongside everyone else when it comes to attitude in the Disability Dynamics (DD) model (Chapter 12).

Success depends on everyone being taken into account.

Carrying on.

Can we be brave, resilient, cheerful, determined etc? For how long? Even if PLUs overcome the bereavement and grief (Chapter 10), there's still all those others' attitudes to cope with (Chapter 12).

Resignation can seem so tempting when others, at best, have no expectation that PLUs have anything to offer, any value, any knowledge or capabilities left, but are just pitiable husks of the people we used to be. Instead, they may be tempted to see us as drains on their energy, compassion and pockets. Giving up could be easy: not making a fuss or too many demands; retiring into the shells of our lives.

I reject the whole concept. Masses of PLUs battle on, finding what we can do and not getting too bothered about what we can't. After all, we weren't going to be brain surgeons before so aren't failures for not being one now.

Chris said: "I have come through prostate cancer, bladder cancer, stomach cancer, collapsed kidney, and next week I go into hospital for surgery to remove throat cancer, followed a couple of weeks later for an operation to remove skin cancer. Got to keep going, so I am still playing golf and playing music to residents in care homes, particularly concentrating on those with dementia and Alzheimer's, and engraving glass, all of which keeps me very busy."

Rebuilding.

In the early days, escaping that trough of depression (Chapter 10) may mean taking little steps along life's new path. Each small challenge overcome makes the next one easier and the route ahead clearer. Even when that step irritatingly and frustratingly fails, we can grudgingly accept it was a 'learning experience' before swiftly moving on. Few PLUs have the capacity to turn our lives around instantaneously and make it a success. Being patient with ourselves can be difficult but may pay off in the longer term.

That former veterinary nurse and I chatted about what might give life more meaning. She was thinking of volunteering with animals (or even people), being creative, mixing more with others, finding some expert advice from charities, Social Services or a job centre. She had the ideas and was working out how to take the next steps. Different paths to different destinations... some could prove worthwhile and others not.

This lady had the potential of most PLUs: highly motivated, socially active, previous work experience, with the will and confidence to want something better from life. Some sensitive back to work support, even some training, and there was someone worth snapping up. But she wasn't an obvious 'low-hanging fruit' offering a quick win but on the start of her journey. Just that bit more help and she'd be on her way rather than facing over 40 years of unwilling benefit dependency.

Working up in Derbyshire, I met many PLUs who'd been out of work for years, often a decade or more, who were still looking forward, motivated and unbroken.

"I felt absolutely awful and completely useless when I wasn't working. I felt I was lumped in with people who are seen as lazy because I have a disability that others don't see." (Anon).

Mental toughness.

There are many ways of describing the right mind-set. Former colleague Nick liked the '4Cs' described by Professor Clough: Control; Commitment; Challenge; Confidence.

1. **Taking Control of your life, circumstances and emotions so that miseries don't distract from what you are doing.**

But having control of life can be challenging for anyone and even worse with a life-changing condition. PLUs often are at the receiving end: medical care; work situations; finances and benefits; domestic situations etc. I suspect many think that they are the ones in charge, that they do things **for** and **to** us, rather than **with** us. Step by step, PLUs need to take back control.

Knowing about all those others' attitudes can help: watch out for the patronising or aggressive (Chapter 12); use your interpersonal skills to get the best out of them; resist being the 'useful' stay-at-home to take in the deliveries and the school-returners.

Be well-informed: researching; listening; reading. We won't be experts in our medical treatment, in equality and employment law, in all the benefit and tax issues, in adaptive technology or other support available, but we can learn and find people who are. Simply 'talking' to others at the clinic, in the waiting room and online can open up new ideas. Every nugget of knowledge is an advantage.

> *As my sight got worse, I learned about screen-reading software for my computer. But I'd need to touch-type rather than the old two-finger method. With free training, and an hour a day one summer month, I learned the basics. Now a keyboard is no mystery, and I can read, write and more.*

Good information and advice help us make decisions and be in control. For example, medical retirement might seem to offer tempting future security but does the money work out if things get worse? What happens to benefits if you want/need to do something more? Think ahead, ask questions, make plans and prepare.

2. Having Commitment in setting yourself goals and getting on with achieving them.

It can be trickier deciding which goal to pursue when there are so many. Choosing between enough money, sound health, a social life, some creativity, work, new adventures and more may be tough. Which comes first and which can be juggled later? What will success look like, so we'll know when we've got it right? It could be as simple as walking to the corner and back or getting a new job with decent pay. Whichever, it doesn't happen in one go but takes time and many steps.

But decisions aren't cast in stone either. Flexibility, willingness to change direction and take shortcuts all help. Again, those early goals may be small ones, but from acorns...

3. Accepting Challenge through relishing the opportunities offered by change and accepting risks.

> *Simon said: "We tend to define ourselves by what we can do. A disability can be seen as diminishing us. Learning and moving forward is a good way to keep the definition of self fluid. The aim is to constantly change what you think is possible."*

Nearly any change can be positive if life is already at rock-bottom. Over-enthusiasm may need sorting by getting well informed and weighing risks. But once a challenge seems reasonable, it's worth energy and dedication: the chance of recovering some of the life we've lost is worth it.

But, at the start, risks may seem overwhelming. We don't want things to get worse for our health, our finances, our relationships, and remaining self-image. Being informed helps keep risks in proportion, identifies the possible dos and definite don'ts. Other people doing things for, to or with PLUs need to help us recognise risk and manage it. If they add more risk of failure, like anyone else we are likely to simply step away. And we need to be the decision-makers, the ones in control.

Inertia can be a tempting trap. Sometimes, simply doing nothing seems easiest because the status quo appears the safest 'comfort zone'. Again, good information and advice helps.

4. Growing Confidence with self-belief and inner strength that can influence others.

> *I suspect that the naval psychiatrist recognised my unbearable ego and stubborn bloody-minded determination. Getting help to get work after the Navy was my top priority as, without income: no mortgage, and no home.*

By the time PLUs have added a couple of other personal goals, we are no longer passive but people with purpose in life again. There are real, practical and important things to do and get on with (and less time for misery).

Of course, there'll be setbacks on the way, things will go wrong, and PLUs need to make changes. But every step of progress and improvement is a success because it shows us what we can do and that we still have control over our lives. The more PLUs do, the stronger we'll get, and make decisions, take action, and move on.

> *Once I was just a naval officer but, since losing my sight, I've done so much more: travelled the world, run a business, survived a near-death accident, written books, and the list goes on. Having a life-changing condition opens up many new, different, and precious forms of success. Even if no one else recognises our triumphs, PLUs know in our hearts.*

Courage.

For PLUs, I'd add another C to Professor Clough's list: Courage. Getting the diagnosis and beginning the treatment is only the start of the struggle. Even if one threat has ended, other miseries often continue, as for Sally with a facial cancer and Nichola after a stroke:

She'd already had to stand, semi-naked and vulnerable behind a tailored lead 'corset' up to her neck while the radiotherapy was fired. I marvel at her courage and fortitude. It seems to have worked but life has certainly changed: taste and smell took years to recover; constantly washing out sinus and nose mucus; teeth irrecoverably damaged and lost; worry about if it will come back.

Nichola's health condition arose following a stroke and ended her career as a slimming consultant. Looking back over the last five years, she said, "I was very miserable and depressed but now I'm managing my health. I've got a purpose to get up in the morning, do something productive and earn some money. I've got my confidence back and know that I'm still capable even though I have illnesses. My family have been brilliant. My husband even helps with the hand-embroidery and fitted out my new business unit. The whole family is happier because I am too."

I listened to someone describing others out of work as 'lazy'. Is that really true? When people can't get jobs, they may face choosing between being labelled ‘unemployable’ or disabled. For many, both can bear the stigma of being worthless, useless or pitiful. Perhaps laziness is preferable. It suggests that an individual still has some agency over their lives: they have chosen not to work. The alternative is publicly acknowledging that they simply have no value because they aren’t able to do a job. Even being deemed a ‘scrounger’ carries that little bit of status of being clever enough to outwit the system. Better that than being worthless.

So what?

More control and confidence can give PLUs the courage and commitment to take on the challenge of making a comeback.

CHAPTER 14.

Do something.

Just starting on this chapter, I came across sociology Professor Corey Keyes of Emory University (USA). He talked about 'languishing' between depression and good mental health. That place where we don't have a mental health condition but also aren't flourishing but feel life is stagnant, empty, without meaning. Perhaps the future appears no more than rather a dull routine of everyday tasks, short on joy, excitement and human contact, repetitive and dull, without much meaning or challenge. Anyone can be languishing, as even a stable family, nice house and good income won't always be enough to make life meaningful and worthwhile.

For PLUs who are struggling with our health, don't have much money, don't get out much, can't get work etc, it may be even easier to slip into languishing. Professor Corey's said, *"Too many people have to suffer the indignities of a society that doesn't send the message that you are useful, and you belong here and we care about you, that you are wanted."*

It all sounds too familiar. Those less-than supportive attitudes that verge between prejudice and discrimination, where PLUs are reduced to economic costs and budget cuts, where we are numbers, not real people. Worsening income inequality sends a strong message that those at the bottom of the pile have little value. No wonder that simply struggling on is exhausting and overwhelming, that some are angry and resentful.

Professor Corey reinforced my ideas about 'doing something' with five distinct suggestions aimed at defiantly proving those negative attitudes wrong.

1. **Be useful.**

Being a do-gooder and helping others becomes more meaningful with a bit of ambition, being proactive rather than passive, adding value that makes the difference. For example, rather than simply buying in the charity shop, give the time and effort to collect for them and even serve at the counter. One thing leads to another: the shop needs a manager, a promotion champion, a trustee. Being useful can progress from doing good to more fulfilment and satisfaction.

There's yet more potential: those new skills, experiences and responsibilities can be translated into a competence-based CV. Most employers want the same things when they recruit: team working, communications, energy, motivation etc. Demonstrating those skills and achievements across different aspects of life can be more persuasive than the dreary standard responsibilities of the 9-to-5 work history.

> *I confess that I started down this do-gooding road for purely selfish reasons. I knew that medical discharge was on the cards and that a CV only covering Navy life wasn't likely to excite many employers. The Hampshire committee of The Prince's Trust was my starting point. Unable to drive, I couldn't get around to talk with the young people needing grants, but I could shuffle paperwork (large font) and keep the meetings on track. As*

the prospects of post-Navy work seemed increasingly impossible, I wanted to focus on helping other PLUs get back to work.

The local Access Group gave me new insights but didn't need anyone new. Instead, together with those county contacts, we created the Diversity Works Partnership with local government bodies, businesses and charities. A bit of funding and our team-working was delivering diversity training to small businesses across south-east England.

PLUs David set up his successful Derbyshire canine exercise business after volunteering and said, "I did some walking for someone else to learn the business and have been volunteering for a local animal sanctuary."

Finally, 'public appointments' often need a PLUs' voice to show their inclusivity. Although such work with government (national and local) is often unpaid, it can offer useful contacts, valuable experience, and looks great on a CV!

Back in 2005, the Cabinet Office was trying to increase PLUs representation in public appointments from a meagre 3-in-100 (hardly reflecting our 1-in-4 of the population!). While reasonable adjustments were often possible, the government bodies had typical recruitment problems: inaccessible information and processes; interviewers with scant understanding of PLUs. Meanwhile, those applicants expected a 'closed shop', their contribution limited to the 'disability voice' and not their wider experience. 'Board-level experience' could put off the most determined applicants when their careers had been disrupted. Life-changing is right. The Public Sector Equality Duty introduced from 2010 may have helped.

Christina was another Navy veteran and still contributed to her local community as a school governor for over five years. "I've always wanted to do something useful for society and, if I can make a difference, it makes me feel that I've done something worthwhile."

2. Learn and grow.

New knowledge and skills can satisfy both mind and soul. Group activities, local courses, online resources, books or just a friend who knows can open up new ideas and fulfil lifelong ambitions.

Not having much money meant I'd always been handy: DIY; painting and decorating; simple electrics. While I could still take the trusty trike to pottery classes and set up a mini studio at home. Together with a great friend, I embarked on decades of flower arranging. The creations have been good enough for many parties, special birthday gifts the wedding and even my mother's funeral. Much better than the standard petrol station bunch.

Grant: I've always been a photographer in my spare time and decided to do it professionally when my previous work became impossible," he explained. "It was two years ago that my partner found me collapsed after a seizure apparently due to some form of brain scarring. Medication means that I can manage the condition, but my previous driving career ended when I lost my licence. While I was recovering, I took college courses to extend my skills and start the business."

On top of new confidence, successful learning in one area is good evidence that the same is possible in others. Just what the job recruiter ordered.

3. Active play.

Paul has been involved in shooting and dog training since he learned from his father on the moors around Doncaster. However, as his partner Denise commented, "We hadn't been able to keep a dog while we were both out working but it was ideal when Paul was at home and ill. We got Salander Sensation, our springer spaniel. Training the dog gave Paul new interest in life and, although he still struggles with his illness, it helped him avoid a really deep depression. In no time, he was helping other people train their own dogs and, as he couldn't go back to his previous work, this was the perfect answer."

"I still need to balance work with my health but now I've made the decision to move forward rather than look back. My physical health has improved with all the fresh air,

walking miles and miles each week, plus less pressure."

Not just the solo round of a game of Patience, but some sort of enjoyable, perhaps physical, activity with other people that causes the excited intake of breath, the heart pumping a bit faster and a shared laugh or cry. Nowadays, with the virtual world at the click of a button or two, many can play games. Others might prefer physical activities, sports, group challenges or traditional card and board games at a community centre or in each other's homes.

I'd always been a swimmer and, in those latter Navy days, had struggled up and down the pool lanes at HMS COLLINGWOOD and the local council leisure centre. Tricky without sight and getting tangled in the lane markers. Aquarobics with friends was more fun, especially when followed by bring-a-dish supper together.

4. Connecting.

It's probably impossible to be helpful, to learn or to play alone. Building those human contacts is much easier when there's a shared purpose too. More connections build more confidence, and those life-changing conditions get pushed into second place.

Paul described his connections with others: "I had to stop working in the iron ore steel industry nearly 15 years ago because of my own health conditions. The years of treatment and recovery were difficult, but it was the effect on my self-confidence that was most crushing. Now I've got through it and want to help others regain their independence too. People need a familiar friendly face with the time to support those normal everyday tasks like dealing with letters, doing the shopping together or pottering around a garden centre. Getting out and mixing with other people is a key part of life – it might be a coffee morning, bingo or a hospital appointment. By having my support throughout, they become much more positive about what they can still do."

"Locally there are very high levels of disabled people and numbers are likely to grow as everyone is living longer. Families and friends aren't always about so a reliable

and empathetic support worker fills the gap. I leave personal care to others but focus on helping people maintain their real quality of life: independence and social links. Helping them avoid the sort of miseries I went through gives me great job satisfaction and the chance to give something back to others." (Anon).

The Welsh National Opera and NHS trialled online singing sessions for PLUs with chronic pain (2025). Early reports suggest that many had less pain, were less isolated and felt more positive about life – though no budding opera stars yet!

I've travelled all around the UK by train and pity those other passengers who simply get on and off in utter isolation. Pitching up at the local station, I'm greeted by Passenger Assistance, who is usually someone I know. We walk, comfortably arm-in-arm, to the platform, chatting about families and the rest of the world. Handed on to the onboard guard, I'm helped to just the right seat and get a few words each time he or she passes. At my destination, there's another familiar voice to greet me by name, offer me an arm and negotiate our way to the front of the taxi queue. One of my most memorable journeys started with the station staff wincing when I accidentally brushed his new tattoo. It became a series of stories over the whole journey as each of my contacts shared their own tales of body art. Other passengers probably registered little more than the uniforms, while I knew what was underneath!

Connecting with other people is usually important when getting a job. Those subtle facial expressions, eye contact (for some), the handshake (for others), the body language, confidence and more all work together at meetings and interviews. We humans are a social species and value others who can connect in real life, not just on social media. In contrast, isolation and loneliness aren't good for anyone and can even increase risk of stroke. Another incentive to connect more!

Recovering in hospital from the latest spinal fracture, I managed to email friends and family. How good and cheering it was to get phone calls back. But not from someone who preferred someone else's interpretation of sympathy rather than troubling to use his thumbs!

5. Spirituality, religion or transcending self.

As a non-believer, this final element of Professor Keyes' theory left me rather bemused until I realised it could also apply to 'Why am I here?'. It is that nebulous meaning of life, the reason for living that is beyond one's own lifespan. What do we bring to the existence of others, past, present or future? What difference has our life made to the world? We will probably never know for sure but can hope that someone, somewhere, has noticed that we existed and made a little difference. Perhaps we gave the right help at the right time to someone, made a connection that was useful, showed another that life as a PLUs still had meaning and value. It's for others to judge but, in our hearts, we may have some clues, some small satisfactions, some reassurance that our existence has had some worth and been noticed.

So what?

Doing something/anything is good for mind, body and soul.

CHAPTER 15.

Back to work principles.

The government's 'Get Britain Working' White Paper outlined their ideas to help more PLUs (and others) to work (2024). The scale of the problem was daunting: "A quarter of all people aged 16 to 64" were PLUs who were "nearly 3 times more likely" than others to be economically inactive. The next year, they followed up with a Green Paper setting out more ideas. It was a curate's egg with some good and less-good bits. My response included early drafts of these chapters.

In a nutshell, strategic back to work answers are more likely to succeed if they are PLUs-centred and collaborative. One government department, one part of society, one sort of driver won't make the difference we all need. Instead, a holistic approach has more potential:

- Abandon the angry, negative words and blame-game. Rather than the easy stereotypes, PLUs are nearly always out of work due to circumstances way beyond our choice or control.

- Include PLUs at every stage so our voices are heard. Representatives are all well and good, but only second-hand input without the persuasive credibility of our actual experience.
- Collaborative partnerships at every level. Combined government (national and local), business and voluntary sectors skills and support could revolutionise what is possible.
- Better, faster healthcare. Targeted and quicker diagnosis, treatment and recovery could avoid the cliff-edge of worklessness.
- Increase chances of keeping-the-job/return-to work. It's not rocket science: the right support and adjustments plus the right carrots and sticks for employers are well known but not well enough used.
- Match action to reality. Like any business proposition, success means understanding 'supply and demand'. If there aren't many job vacancies, PLUs chances will be less too. Likewise, 'customer-focused' action means understanding PLUs' reality: fragile motivation/confidence, less marketable age/skill profiles, accessibility needs in the widest sense plus myriad other challenges.

When half of PLUs already work, more is easily possible.

Push at the open door of enterprise. Self-employment and business support, policies and practices tailored to budding PLUs entrepreneurs offers even more success. Again, the reality of more working PLUs taking this route than others show what is possible.

- Embed accessibility (in the broadest sense) throughout. After all, if the government departments making the laws don't comply with them, why should anyone else?
- Celebrate success. Complete the full circle with positive stories replacing the negative, changing 'hearts and minds', celebrating success for all.

A final thought: small is beautiful. There's been lots of enthusiasm for a few, very large back to work contracts in the past, whether with private or voluntary sector organisations. Even if they are 'not-for-profit', lots of the funding can disappear into the organisation itself rather than directly helping PLUs. Smaller teams with the right motivation may be more cost-effective and more successful.

So what?

Achieving fulfilment of PLUs potential needn't be difficult: better 'hearts and minds' approach for everyone involved; more focus on employers' responsibilities; recognition that enterprise can be a winner; more cross-departmental working (DWP, health, education, business, HMRC, justice, ETS, ACAS and probably more).

CHAPTER 16.

Keeping the job.

The Royal Navy changed my life. No, not the obvious stuff of having a great career, travel, promotion, new opportunities, super colleagues, tradition and history. Even more important, the Navy made it possible for me to keep working as I lost my sight. The massive steroid treatment couldn't save my right eye and was damaging both kidneys and liver. It took 14 months off work to recover enough to get back into uniform. A new job and new prospects but, all too soon, the left eye was going too and there was no realistic remedy.

But, in the meantime, I'd made Commander (three thick gold stripes) and was given charge of the headquarters of Flag Officer Surface Flotillas (basically, all the ships). Traditionally, 'The Commander' of an establishment swank around with a black, silver-topped cane. Mine was just white and collapsible.

A great team of military and civilian people, adaptive software plus large print documents meant I could still do the job. I moved on to the Old Naval Academy in the Portsmouth dockyard, revising the appraisal system for about 37,000 people. I could move around, carrying my uniform tricorn hat to avoid any saluting and relying on the security guards to fish me out of the bushes.

With medical discharge on the horizon, I feared no work, no income, no mortgage, no home, but those years proved to me that I could still do a good job, and that blindness wasn't the end of the world. That self-confidence was the key to the future and a precious gift from the Navy.

In contrast, during those years, I remember the civil servant who had increasing problems getting around. The possibility of 'reasonable adjustments' to help him didn't seem to have been considered. Instead, he was grateful to get 'medical retirement' when another job was a remote prospect.

Benefits and pension at least offered some future security.

But David was emphatic that giving up work due to ill health was the wrong decision and said, "Taking 'medical retirement' is the worst thing you can do and the greatest mistake of my life. You just feel worthless and end up watching daytime television. My marriage went through a rocky period, and I was losing friends by being so self-absorbed. I hated the life I had and couldn't stand it any longer."

In recent times, the economy has suffered the loss of nearly three million workless PLUs' experience, productivity, spending power and taxes. Alongside, others have dropped out of work and the population is aging. Add some 1.5 million over-50 PLUs to the recent bulge of around 1.2 million younger PLUs, and we've a major challenge for all our economic futures.

The Law.

Employers have responsibilities to make reasonable adjustments for their people who have life-changing conditions. These can include adaptive equipment, accessible workplaces, a different job and more but most costing employers nothing or very little. Yet many workers and their employers seem unable to resolve the situations together. Instead, jobs and futures are lost while employers risk employment tribunals with all the associated costs, time and reputational damage. After all, if that employer is breaking one law, what else are they doing wrong?

Keeping the job challenges.

> *After six years as a Sapper motor mechanic in the Royal Engineers, David worked with the RAC on vehicle recovery but said, "After four years, I wanted a change from laying in the snow mending exhausts." He spent a year driving buses, but ill health intervened and he has spent the next seven years being unable to work due to recurring health problems. "It was a bit of a blow to lose that job. I decided that I would never work for an employer again because of how I was treated when I was ill. I tried to do odd jobs, but my health was getting in the way."*

Time passes.

Many of us will be working when that health condition arises, often from middle age onwards. Getting the GP and consultant appointments, tests and scans, diagnosis, treatment and whatever recovery is possible all seem to take far too long and puts jobs at risk. Employers may cope with the cost of those off sick in the short term but, understandably, are concerned with the bottom line. They may simply not know what to do, how to make adjustments or the legal risks they are running. Not surprisingly, many PLUs slide through the revolving door from short-term to long-term sick with all the consequent future problems of getting another job.

One or more?

For some, one condition just isn't enough. More emerge: about 3-in-10 working aged people had multiple conditions; nearly a million had five or more; over 1-in-10 (about five million) had some level of depression or anxiety. Yet, lots are proud to be working still.

What could hold us back?

Even with treatment, there's the obvious: that life-changing condition itself; physical/mental fluctuations; the impact of treatment. But there's often more. The influence of family, friends, wider society and the work 'system' all play their part. Yet most PLUs -in -the-making are highly motivated to keep the reality they know (the job, the life, the income). The alleged 'easy' route of 'learned helplessness' is more often pushed on us by others.

Changing their and reinforcing our 'hearts and minds' before work is lost is key. Trying to mend broken aspirations with off-the-shelf, bake-and-shake CV-writing/job-search approaches 'after the fact' is much more difficult.

Ignorance and isolation.

Meanwhile, fellow workers usually want to be supportive. But they may not understand what's happening or how best to help when its more than the usual flu or sprain. They don't want to risk adding pressure. Often doing nothing seems easiest and safest. But just losing contacts, confidence and daily work routines while tackling that health problem can be a blow to self-respect, motivation and determination. Worse if the 'system' doesn't seem to care. The lure of a different, poorer future may seem easier than battling across the medical, work and financial fronts.

> *While I was off sick for all those months, it took emergency hospital admissions before any 'official' contact. Not a great feeling of being valued or even missed a bit.*

At the same time, new PLUs may know little about employment rights, what to do, who to ask and how to manage the journey back to work. Different 'expectations' on all sides might be more positive as suggested by the RF's 'right to return'.

> *I spent some years amidst the leading players of ACAS, the judiciary and the ETS as a member of the ET System Steering Board. I championed the needs of fellow PLUs in negotiating the process, standing up for themselves at a tribunal and challenging the potential unfair dismissals. But surprisingly, there was resistance to providing ACAS and*

tribunal information in Jobcentres where PLUs would be seeking help. Perhaps things have changed.

Bosses need help too.

Many line managers don't know enough about their legal responsibilities and have even less capacity to fulfil them. Often, they're already juggling priorities. Many don't know that most working PLUs need no or no-cost workplace adjustments and that there's help from the government's Access to Work (ATW) scheme too. There are extra bonuses: keeping a valuable experienced worker saves replacement recruitment and training costs while bolstering reputation across the organisation and with customers. The fact that half of PLUs still hold down jobs busts the 'too costly, too risky, taking too much time off' myths.

Work risks.

Some types of jobs seemed more likely to shed PLUs according to post-Covid data: more from wholesale and retail followed by transport and storage, hospitality, health and social work, construction and manufacturing. Although some were doubtless harder hit by the pandemic's economic consequences, many were more likely to have had PLUs employees in the first place. Thumbs up to all those employers.

In contrast, some jobs (information and communication, public administration, scientific and some professional and managerial occupations) shed fewer PLUs but, probably, had les at the start. Keeping/getting-the-job initiatives might do well by targeting the right employers.

Strategic consequences.

Whatever the reasons, more PLUs leaving work increases risk for economic growth. There will be less taxes to collect, more benefits to pay and less productivity. Overseas workers, AI and changed work practices may be needed to fill gaps. Deprived areas may suffer worse while the national reputation flags.

Policymakers are already looking at new approaches for large-scale success. But past experience of coercive benefit sanctions, ruthless job application-by-rote regimes, focus on easy-to-place 'low-hanging fruit' plus some disability-conscious employers are unlikely to cut the mustard.

So what?

Circumstances beyond our control, rather than choice, can tip PLUs into worklessness. Building on existing relationships with employers is the starting point.

CHAPTER 17.

Back to work: where we are now.

In the late 90s, I couldn't imagine how I'd work when, inevitably, I'd have to leave the Navy. There didn't seem to be any help other than one ex-Service charity suggesting a future as a 'library researcher'. They didn't quite realise the meaning of blindness! Another charity seemed to think that offering a nice lunch would do the job.

I'd spotted a gap in the market: helping other PLUs to get back to work. Never one to be shy or unassuming, I still wanted to be in control of my life. But I needed more than bravado to be convincing.

That volunteering with The Prince's Trust produced invaluable contacts and a reality check on life in 'Civvy Street'. After all, I'd never held down a job in the real world.

But where to start looking for paid work? Back then, we didn't have social media to strut our stuff or find opportunities (even if we could see). Instead, it was the old-fashioned phone call to anyone in PLUs-world. Some I knew, but most were cold calls that needed a thick skin. Imagine this strange blind woman ringing out of the blue. I quickly learned that asking for advice rather than help was best. People were much more willing if they didn't have to make any commitment or take any responsibility.

With time, I had the start of a network and was narrowing the work field. My luck held out: my first paid consultancy work started just a couple of days after taking off uniform in 1999 and, within a year, committed to PLUs employment, I launched Disability Dynamics Ltd.

(It sounds all too easy looking back when I had a Service pension to fall back on; but together with the new earnings, I could keep my home. Nearly as important, I had a new purpose that made life meaningful.)

What's changed over the last quarter century?

During the early 2000s and into the teens, there had been some reduction in the 'disability employment' gap: the difference between the proportions of working-age PLUs and others in jobs. Good news that more PLUs were working, though more often part-time or self-employed, in less secure jobs and on lower pay.

Since then, we've had a financial crisis, austerity, Brexit, Covid and more hits on the economy and workforce. Nevertheless, more people were in jobs and there were more vacancies too. But PLUs weren't doing so well at getting those jobs. It was like stepping back into the mid-90s. Yet the benefits were obvious: more PLUs filling those vacancies, having more money to spend and save, better pensions, less reliance on benefits and better lives. Win-win.

What's on the horizon?

There's a risk of more workless PLUs. There was a bulge of under-35-year-olds (according to the 2021 Census). Nearly another half million children may be in the pipeline facing long waits for diagnosis, treatment and support. The prospective worker-pool may get even smaller when the record-breaking drop in birth rates feeds through. An under-class-in-the-making, with direct consequences for all. Policymakers, employers and everyone may learn that PLUs count towards the pluses and minuses of the national economy and the undercurrent of contentment (or not).

What's been tried?

Regarding practical support and survival, toughening up the benefits system seemed simple but doesn't appear to have made the difference. Sanction target tales of phantom vacancies, appointments impossible to attend and more have rocked the DWP reputation.

The UN was *'appalled'* by the level of benefit deaths of PLUs *"resorting to suicide following the denial of an adequate standard of living and social protection"* that risks breach of international law. If the powers-that-be aren't on our side, who is?

More positively, in 2023, the DWP reported on the Work and Health programme. Over its five years, about 300,000 PLUs had taken part and about 3-in-10 had reached the target earnings threshold or six months self-employment. Worsening health or existing skills not being transferrable doubtless played a part for some. Fear and risk-aversion amongst both PLUs and employers probably contributed too, but the score card probably still says, *'Could do better'.*

What's getting in the way?

One size doesn't fit all. PLUs' odds are even worse when other diversity factors are added to the mix. Ethnic background (Arab, Black, Asian), younger/older, sex, location and qualifications all work against us. For example, it seems that recruiters may ignore anyone in their late 50s.

There's evidence from other fields that stereotypes and stigma easily creep into attitudes, decision-making and the systems that drive our lives. In medicine, for example, much research has been male-orientated and long-held beliefs determined that some races had higher pain thresholds. Like treatments that ignore the conditions of many, recruitment and back to work systems that don't reflect reality are equally doomed.

The automated systems, checklists, data predeterminants, access to our personal data and bank accounts all tend to reduce us to numbers, not people. Add the distinct possibilities of inherent bias in Artificial Intelligence for more risk. When we PLUs can't tick their boxes, we may be on a hiding to nothing without a whole system reset.

What would help.

At the government policy level, let's avoid silo thinking but have a cross-departmental strategy that is practical, realistic and caring. Good effective fast solutions might be more persuasively productive than bullying PLUs who already feel marginalised.

On the health front, new prevention steps may only bring change in the long term. Meanwhile, getting the tests, diagnosis and treatment sorted fast, getting any adaptations in place pronto can help our PLUs get back to the lives they know and want. If we can cope with a pregnancy or male mid-life crisis, other health conditions needn't be that different.

Active job/worker retention by employers would pay dividends in keeping talent and experience, avoiding recruitment/training costs and building reputation. Making access to employment tribunals rather more possible would flex the stick. A sensible, pragmatic society would realise that the workforce needs as many people as possible. Women are already getting better chances, so let's do the same for PLUs (and many others). It may not be equality yet, but a start.

For those slipping through the cracks, earlier help from the planned Jobcentre/Careers Service combo might offer more realistic practical help and support, re-training, accessibility and employment rights, different ways of working and ATW. And, while developing that better support, we shouldn't forget the millions already languishing on benefits. Starting with motivated volunteers could show those less confident that there are still chances in life.

> *Steve said, "I wasn't able to work for nearly two years due to my health. One day I came*

in from the garden dripping with blood but didn't know how I'd cut my arm. After lots of tests, I was eventually diagnosed with non-epileptic attack disorder that had been causing blackouts of which I was never aware. My wife was at least pleased to know what had been going on for years as she had thought I was ignoring her when, in reality, I just didn't know that the blackouts were happening. Relying on benefits was horrible after a successful career as a telecommunications retail manager. I wanted to work but couldn't, so my anxiety got worse, which caused more blackouts. I'd applied for many jobs and even got some interviews, but found them very stressful which impacted on my health. So I decided on self-employment so that I could control my environment, work and deadlines. Now I get up in the morning and look forward to work, which is even better when customers love what I do. My health has improved too: I haven't had any attacks for over a year and have even got my driving licence back. My relationships with my wife and kids are so much better."

Having said all of which, at the heart of future thinking, the financial benefits of a stronger economy may be more convincing than any diversity logic.

Footnote.

Pensions shouldn't be forgotten either. Apocryphal data suggests that many in more physical, manual jobs suffer more wear and tear while often having limited alternative work prospects. Perhaps they should retire earlier (like some other countries) to nurse their health and remaining years. However, new health hazards may be developing with screen time, social media, processed food and other consequences of modern life. Those decision-makers may need to balance the risk of universal eligibility, such as State pension age, against the cost and divisiveness of tailored systems.

Further delay of State pension age to, say, 70 might work for some. On the other hand, those who can afford it may already have stopped work and, as the data shows, about half will be PLUs by then. Better lifetime health due to less poverty, healthier lifestyles, safer work and more transferrable skills are probably needed before retirement age tinkering is worthwhile. Cross-governmental ideas may have little traction when the benefits are so far beyond the electoral cycle.

So what?

With more PLUs out there than most of us probably realise, there are better ways of tapping into all the lost potential. Everyone benefits: PLUs, our communities, wider society and our economy.

CHAPTER 18.

Back to work: hearts and minds.

Touchy-feely stuff.

Attitudes, emotions and psychology should be at the heart of new and more successful support. In reality, very many PLUs would like jobs, need the income and seek life that is as 'normal' as possible. Instead, take the depression and anxiety felt by anyone losing their work status and pay, then multiply the consequences by being a PLUs too. When healthcare doesn't resolve a condition, keeping remnants of self-respect and avoiding further 'failure' may be more important than endlessly submitting hopeless sanction-driven job applications.

Fear and stigma.

Unlike those who wield the white cane or drive their chairs, most PLUs have 'hidden' disabilities. A whole mix of attitudes and emotions may make many reluctant to acknowledge their situation to themselves, let alone their employers.

The UN talked of those with *"fear of actual or perceived stigma and may be reluctant to request adaptations at work"*.

Without the likelihood of a sympathetic, supportive and practically helpful response, they're more likely to Keep Mum and miss out on the adjustments they need.

Health-driven.

Apathy may be a symptom of neurogenerative illnesses such as Parkinson's and depression but can also result from other situations. For example, it is well known that people who see themselves on the bottom rungs of life can be less motivated as their dopamine levels are lower. Others with high levels of anxiety face a vicious circle of perceived threats, indecision and avoidance through inactivity. Pessimism founded on past 'failures' can be a strong driver of inaction: what's the point of trying when all your experience is of helplessness in avoiding misery and disappointment? Self-protective inertia maybe one's only form of control.

Change.

Successful back to work offers will reduce anxiety and threat, offer realistic prospect of success, graduate risk levels in line with growing self-confidence and so strengthen motivation. There's simply no value in any step that reinforces apathy.

> *Our mantra in the back to work field was "We've got one chance to get it right." PLUs who'd been told they can't work by their GPs, previous employers, friends and families, other employers and even the benefits system, tend to believe it. Yet many still have hope, ambition, motivation and determination to reach a fulfilling life.*
>
> *Our job was to build on that resilience so those individuals could achieve the first*

steps of their future potential. That often meant rebuilding confidence, refocussing existing skills and fostering new ones.

Some would inevitably withdraw as health and other life circumstances demanded, but we could forecast success for about 4-in-10. Even those who had to drop out could do so with dignity, knowing what was available and able to return when possible.

Over-promising would have been as destructive as bullying or pressurising. When people have already faced one life-changing situation, they are right to tread lightly on another. Failure is bad enough for anyone, worse when it's a repeat. Worse still when it happens despite the help of 'professionals'. There are only so many knock-backs and 'failures' that already damaged self-respect can survive.

Already lost?

Spare more than a thought for the 7-in-10 (over 200,000) who didn't get through those years of the Government Work Programme. For many, yet another 'failure' that's unlikely to persuade them to try again, meaning the programme probably entrenched their worklessness. ONS data offers an eery echo: over 7-in10 PLUs said they weren't interested in getting back to work.

Those delivering the benefits systems and back to work support would do well to remember that they are dealing with already fragile lives and must avoid doing further damage.

No voice.

Shifting attitudes isn't easy when PLUs are under-represented amongst all those who make the important decisions in Parliament, all those public bodies (national and local), throughout business and the voluntary sector. Many may be well-meaning and personally supportive but still don't drive through positive, practical change. Equality and employment law doesn't seem to make much difference either.

Even if strong leadership, good management, and ethics could increase PLUs employment, it probably won't happen unless the 'bottom line' benefits too. So far, no one's shown the data, counted the money or proved the case well enough to change decades of prejudice.

It's not surprising that PLUs prefer to keep our heads down and avoid any more risk. We still punch below our weight. If any other quarter of the population stood up to be counted, the politicians would probably take note and more action. Disability charities, the EHRC etc are great comfort blankets of representation but haven't yet made the changes we need.

So what?

Successful future back to work ideas will tackle the anxiety, fear, depression and stigma PLUs face. Most life-changing conditions won't go away, but our sense of 'failure' and others' negative reactions can.

CHAPTER 19.

Back to work: The early years.

Unlike the 'outside' world, the Royal Navy seemed safe and supportive. I'd pursued ambitions with barely a thought for how others could be struggling. Losing my sight brought me up short, confronted by my own ignorance and the prejudice and discrimination, the sheer lack of compassion that PLUs face. Few of us have much idea about how to get back to work and even less when it's complicated by a health condition. Workless and struggling with health and money problems is a difficult time to start learning.

At the start of the century, as a brand new, self-styled 'disability consultant', I worked with the then Benefits Agency and Employment Service (since joyfully combined into Jobcentre Plus) on their Keeping in Touch project. In those distant days, PLUs deemed unable to work were generally consigned to Incapacity Benefit and had little other contact with government agencies. The project wanted to check if people were getting the right money and, importantly, whether any might get back to work.

Around the same time, I was part of a New Deal for Disabled People project delivering a novel back to work approach for PLUs in Hampshire. The concept was simple: gather small groups of unemployed PLUs; give them more motivation and skills; put them back on the road to work.

What we did.

Keeping in Touch.

The project team contacted over 800 local Southampton PLUs receiving IB by letter, phone or visit. Where contact did succeed, benefit situations were checked and ambitions for work explored. A few went on to meetings with the Employment Service.

New Deal for Disabled People.

PLUs answered simple adverts for the introductory bonding day where the PLUs team ran motivational activities. Another four days focussed on essential positive mind-sets: self- confidence and esteem; positive attitudes; visualising success; assertiveness; change management; goal setting and persistence. Four weeks of phone coaching around individuals' goals followed. The group re-gathered for two more days of key support information such as ATW, permitted work, self-employment, job search, CV writing, career profiling and interview techniques with more help offered by local training, employment and recruitment agencies. The final celebration marked everyone's progress.

What we learned.

Keeping in Touch.

Perhaps most striking, it became clear that no official had been in touch with many of those PLUs for a very long time. This was obvious when about half the phone calls failed.

Benefits were still being paid but the PLUs had been disconnected, changed their numbers or simply weren't answering. Nowadays, the DWP probably has better connectivity.

There wasn't much to learn on the benefits front. Few had any changes to feedback. As to future work aspirations, most were distressed by their seemingly hopeless prospects. They didn't like the stigma of disability but preferred to think of themselves as 'being off sick'. Even amongst those who'd been thinking about work for some time, few had done anything. They were too wary, saying "*There should be something to fall back on should it go wrong.*" They didn't want to be pigeon-holed, but current finances and future security were their top priorities.

There were new insights for the officials too: health limitations; psychological constraints (wariness and lack of confidence); practical barriers (low qualifications; limited work experience; need for training); the problems of navigating job searches (not knowing what to do, who to contact); how to plan finances, negotiate through bureaucracy and overcome employers' attitudes. The very few who dipped their toes in the Employment Service Pond floundered, perhaps because the staff were so unprepared to assist PLUs who were easier to categorise as 'not ready for work' or 'only part-time work applicable'.

Good empathetic human-to-human contact with clear simple information might have broken down PLUs' fears and officials' preconceptions. For some PLUs, simply going into an official building was a daunting prospect yet, played right, the officials were pushing at an open door.

PLUs said the project was *"A really good idea" and "A crucial thing to do".* Those officials were equally positive, saying *"excellent", "marvellous",* and, tellingly, *"took away the fear".* Direct interactions had also challenged some of their assumptions about PLUs claimants as they said, "*There are a lot more genuine people*", very few were defrauding the benefit system, and only some were receiving everything to which they were entitled.

There seemed to be a strange idea that back to work interventions weren't worthwhile within six months of a benefit claim. Yet, in many cases, the PLUs would have been off work for some time even before their job was ended. Instead of inspiring them early, the policy was more likely to increase their distance from work.

> *You can imagine my preferred approach: sitting next to someone in that imaginary hospital bed, waiting for the anaesthetic to wear off and so make the best of their motivation and confidence before the world of work faded.*

Overall, there wasn't anything surprising, though useful lessons reinforced the value of rapport and trust, of communicating well, of support grounded in real understanding of PLUs and, most of all, of outcomes geared to real people rather than just short-term targets.

New deal for disabled people.

Simple low-cost advertising through local media and PLUs groups revealed demand beyond our capacity. Everyone was a volunteer and even those who'd been out of work for over five years were still motivated and responding.

Joining in didn't mean a form-filling challenge but a simple phone call. Other information was straightforward and accessible rather than a dreary series of handouts. Money matters were important. Help with travel removed one difficulty while many needed immediate expert advice about their finances, benefits and debt.

For those often lonely and isolated, getting out of the house for group activities amidst good hospitality was an attractive return to more 'normal' life. The person-centred approach worked. PLUs-to-PLUs interactions reinforced motivation and confidence that built towards harder back to work practicalities.

Severity and/or multiple health conditions wasn't the drawback for most and few thought that they weren't 'fit for work'. If they weren't sure already, they learned that the disability label didn't have to mean incapable. Taking part for one had *"Made me realise just how employable I am."*

Although a few dropped out, most carried on, their aspirations and knowledge growing. But they also realised that the next work steps might be beyond their control. One wanted *"help to get a foot in the door – I'm capable after the first break,"* and another needed to *"let employers know that I can do a job despite being out of work for a while."*

The external training, employment and recruitment agencies (at that time) weren't reassuring that they could bridge the gap between ambitious PLUs and cautious employers. Their funding limitations, business priorities, reputational worries and sheer lack of knowledge about PLUs-potential restricted their offer. There was a risk that the attendees' hopes and aspirations had been raised, only to be dashed when 'pigeon-holed' rather than being seen for their capabilities. The old Employment Service didn't fare much better. Experience was that they *"don't listen to you and what you want"* and *"want you to do any job that is going."*

The subsequent 2010 Equality Act should have made a difference although rising numbers of workless PLUs suggests not enough. Overall, there was much ambition to be honed and tapped once immediate financial worries were resolved. Both back to work agencies and employers needed better understanding of the business benefits of a broader workforce.

Nevertheless, the Switch on to Success model had been born and was triumphantly rolled out around the country for years to come by my (then) colleagues Nick and Stephen.

So what?

It's too easy to under-estimate PLUs' potential, motivation and ambition. Likewise, to ignore our skills, insight and capacity to lead and deliver that change. A marriage made in heaven once policymakers realise they don't always know best.

CHAPTER 20.

Back to work: team effort.

In the late 1990s, on the brink of leaving the Navy, I realised that I knew virtually nothing about 'real' life. Getting another job, possibly benefits and all the other sorts of help available for PLUs was a mystery.

Nowadays, there is indeed a huge amount of information and help on the internet. But not so fast. It can still be overwhelmingly daunting to wade through all that information even if we have all the right kit and connections, and it is accessible (but not very with screen-reader software). Add the life-changing health situation, job loss and all the accompanying worries, plus anxiety, despair and fragile motivation.

My first foray into team-working was leading the Diversity Works Partnership, bringing together Hampshire county plus Portsmouth and Southampton city councils, local businesses (such as Ford) plus voluntary organisations working in the south of the county.

Years later, Bolsover District Council asked me to create a partnership of all the local organisations supporting PLUs back to work. I suspect that they anticipated a dozen or so ranging from the Jobcentre to specialist charities. They'd probably forgotten that other organisations offering services to the public have a legal duty to make reasonable adjustments for PLUs and many were keen to both improve and promote their help. The upshot was the Help to Work partnership of over 50 organisations (public, business and voluntary) all contributing something to the back to work journey (financial budgeting, health improvement, upskilling, job search, self-employment and more. That concept went on to become one of just six projects in Europe to gain EU funding and test partnership working in practice.

What we did.

Diversity Works Partnership.

Pooling our ideas aimed to make work more attainable for many marginalised people across South Hampshire. Prejudice about age, disability, ethnicity, religion and more needed to be overcome for so many and partners had all the background and knowledge needed. We built on their own specialist and practical diversity skills, sharing ideas through regular meetings. Alongside, partners' own in-house specialists created the Diversity Trainers group to share expertise and practical delivery tips. Everyone learned from each other. Our Diversity Works project also shared knowledge with small- and medium-size businesses across south-east England through workplace training and a straightforward equality 'manual'.

Help To Work.

The basis was the numerous organisations (some disability specialists, some not) operating in part of Derbyshire. Partners included the obvious back to work players (Jobcentre staff, recruitment agencies, self-employment business advisers, CV gurus and more), but we also realised that PLUs needed much broader holistic help from health and money matters (for many) to addiction and ex-offender support (for a few). Health providers stepped up, wanting to know more about the longer-term impact of the conditions they treated. Likewise, practical financial help was often vital so that those on tight budgets could better manage their debts, claim their benefit entitlements and put food on the table. (It seems obvious, but those too strapped for cash have more problems doing all the back to work steps that require online access, travel costs and even the right clothes.)

Collectively, we created the 'Steps to Success' back to work map based on Maslow's Hierarchy of Needs (Annex A). With some 50 local, regional and national partner organisations covering that huge range of needs, the online directory of partners' key information meant everyone (and the public too) could easily find what was on offer. Regular meetings, training, conference, briefings, speed-dating events and newsletters all gave partners time and space to learn about each other's skills and build trust.

Confident of positive progress for PLUs, we also created the 'Flexicurity' model (following the Maslow principles) to make new jobs and work progress more successful (Annex B).

What we learned.

Diversity Works Partnership.

Partners already knew about some workplace equality issues and learned even more from each other and the training. Importantly, mixing front-line with policy/ management people produced new joined-up thinking for all.

Small and medium-sized businesses often knew that they lacked the equality awareness needed for employees and customers. Our energetic promotion unleashed their latent demand; The training was delivered at their locations by the different partners with the manual to provide longer-term information.

Help To Work.

A key theme was avoiding a 'sausage factory' approach not suited to diverse clients facing diverse problems. Instead, the further PLUs (and others) were from work, the more they needed personal, local, specialist and holistic help that the partnership, rather than single providers, could supply. Partners knew who else could fill the gap and had the personal understanding and trust to refer vulnerable clients for the extra support. Together, there was more chance of achieving work success.

Friendly, relaxed partner meetings broke down barriers, shared expertise and reinforced the prospects of joint working for everyone's benefit. Training for partners increased their PLUs understanding and 'buy-in' to the jointly created models, the directory and better delivery and outcomes for clients.

The fly in the ointment was the variety of funding regimes that directly conflicted with partnership working. There were different data and IT systems, outcome and evidence requirements, eligibility criteria, funding durations and much more. While organisations were keen to work with each other, those regimes got in the way. Partnership working was needed between commissioning and funding bodies too, whether national or local.

So what?

Designing the 'What' needed by employers and PLUs isn't difficult but the 'How' of delivery is trickier. Partnerships working together, with shared ambitions, have better chances of succeeding for everyone.

CHAPTER 21.

Back to work: self-employment.

How stupid can one be? After years helping other PLUs get jobs, I'd completely overlooked the obvious.

In 2005 I was invited to help a tiny not-for-profit organisation (Business Ability Ltd) to promote self-employment for PLUs. The full revelation came the following year at a European Blind Union (EBU) conference in Cyprus. As one of the UK delegates, I was talking about the real-life blind working people who featured on the EBU website. Even that should have given me a clue! But listening to speakers from across Europe, South Africa and Japan about others working as beekeepers, vegetable growers, lawyers, musicians, coffin-makers, masseurs and more, the penny finally dropped. Self-employment, entrepreneurship, micro-businesses, sole traders – whatever the term – here was a solution that offered PLUs control of work locations, hours, activities and much more.

A chance meeting with Margaret Hodge, then the Minister for Employment, made it clear that we'd need to prove the concept before the chance of any funding. Together with the Business Ability professionals, we turned their knowledge and experience into a delivery manual and found some cash from the East Midlands Development Agency to run a nine-month pilot across Derbyshire.

But Business Ability didn't have the finances to underwrite the experiment. Instead, I put my own money where my mouth was with a personal loan to DD to cover the risks and responsibilities. Even then, we still had stiff competition to get the contract. Some you win: our first Work for Yourself (WFY) programme rolled out in 2007. More tightly funded projects followed, focussing on the ex-mining deprivation, unemployment and disability hotspot areas of Chesterfield and Bolsover councils. Although the mine closures had taken place years before, the concept of 'legacy trauma' and inter-

generational problems in isolated but tight-knit communities deprived of their main income stream was evident.

During those years, about half the clients were on the main disability benefits (Employment and Support Allowance or Incapacity Benefit), nearly 3-in-10 on Job Seeker's Allowance or Income Support, and many were getting other public-funded help too. There were some good savings to be had for the 'public purse'.

What we did.

Recruitment and service-delivery.

Once again, motivated volunteers responded to local newspaper 'Situations Vacant' adverts that focussed on health conditions (downplaying the dreaded D-word). Every client deserved top notch customer service, courtesy, respect and flexibility. Throughout, we aimed to respond quickly, take account of accessibility needs at every stage, and monitor service frequency and satisfaction.

Business support.

The first one-to-one meeting with their personal, qualified and experienced Business Adviser (John or Nicky) usually took place where the client was comfortable (often their own home or a local café or library). We wanted to build essential rapport and empower clients to progress at their own pace, recognising that health could add delays.

We'd reduced the concept of business to basic elements:

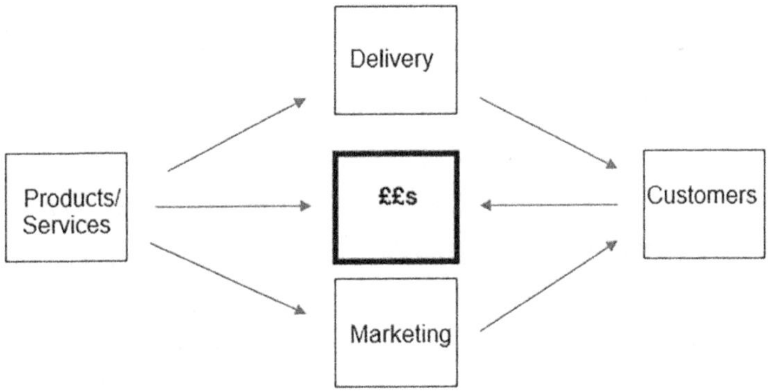

These were expanded through more one-to-one meetings, phone calls and emails, supporting clients to progress through their business development: idea, market research, financial planning and record-keeping, marketing and delivery, de-mystifying business jargon on the way. For example, 'market testing' can sound like a black art, but is only asking the right people the right questions.

> *One client aiming to open a shop for local fishing enthusiasts had been around all the local ponds asking the fishermen what bait they used. I remember his rather frantic phone call once his shop was open. The electricity was down, the fridges off and his bait maggots had escaped!*

The test is whether there will be enough customers willing to pay enough money for the product often enough for the idea to be worthwhile.

> *Stephen had an original way of checking out the market and potential competition. After a heart attack and triple bypass surgery, his survival prospects were slim according to the doctor. Rather than burden his wife, Stephen decided to arrange his own funeral but was dismayed by what was on offer. "I wanted people who would be sensitive to my situation*

> *and that would show me some care and respect. But this was not always the case. The whole experience showed me that there is a niche in the market for funeral services that really care and that cater for different levels of cost."*

Self-employment needs various formalities such as registering with HMRC, setting up bank accounts, getting insurance and more. The skill was in shaping all this knowledge and information into a package that worked for clients. All the business information was obviously available in alternative formats, but basic straightforward readability was equally essential, avoiding various officialese and financial jargon.

Having built client confidence through the individual meetings and, with their business ideas progressing, we knew that these budding entrepreneurs needed to interact happily with new people and potential customers. We added group sessions for those nearing business launch: simple record-keeping to help manage finances; an excellent session on tax delivered by HMRC staff; the 'Confidence with Customers' workshop; marketing seminars.

And all backed up with straightforward accessible step-by-step workbooks.

Our press releases for every new business put the entrepreneurs on the map.

> *Business adviser, John, said, "Something as straightforward as the prospect of seeing your name and achievement in the local paper can be a huge boost. The clients gain self-esteem and can be further motivated by such recognition. All of this is especially important when they are taking the decisive step to relinquish benefits and set out on their own."*

Funding was stretched tight so we could offer some nine months help for each client up to business launch (although many progressed faster) and further support throughout the first year of trading.

Economic background.

The WFY projects had started by the time of the 2008 economic crisis and ran on into 2015. During those years, local Business

Links had been replaced with a website and call centre. OK for some but not necessarily PLUs. One national charity helped young entrepreneurs but didn't understand 'reasonable adjustments. Another catered for PLUs but help was few and far between. New Enterprise Allowance (NEA) was extended from Jobseeker's Allowance (JSA) claimants (over 2-in-10 PLUs then) to the main disability benefits (ESA and IB). Although the NEA timescales were tight, collaborative working meant clients could get the NEA benefits alongside the WFY business support.

By late 2013, there was some economic recovery. Self-employment had increased nationally, supported by NEA, and as those who'd lost jobs or retired 'early' turned to enterprise to improve their incomes. Jobcentres were reporting fewer JSA claimants, had problems filling vacancies, 'Return to Work' payments had stopped and sanctions increased. Yet the improvements didn't always reach everyone: *"People with a disability and those aged 50 and over are the least successful in getting a job through the Work Programme"* (Centre for Social and Economic Inclusion).

Meanwhile, WFY was plugging on and looking for the next opportunity. But, in 2014, my own long battle with DWP started and, without the ATW support I needed to work, I couldn't take the risk of underwriting the next contract. Disability Dynamics could no longer function.

What we learned.

Level of demand.

We were pushing at an open door. We could achieve all our targets during just eight months a year (school holidays weren't worth the advertising). In reality, there was even more demand, but we had to decline about 1-in-5 because they were out of our funding area. Alongside, partnership working with other local organisations produced dividends: more client referrals and a wider network of support for them. There was no shortage of PLUs volunteering for a chance to work.

> *"I wanted to get off benefits: I get bored and need to be doing something."* And, *"After being on benefits for years, I was getting fed*

up being at home so I thought I would use the skills I had gained in the past."

Clients.

Most were in middle age or older with valuable work and life experiences, though often less formal educational qualifications. Yet, about 1-in-3 hadn't worked for two years or more. For some, their old skills and experience no longer matched their changed capabilities.

Ian's building career ended with multiple fractures in a car accident. Despite restricted movement in one hand and limited mobility, he didn't want to live on social security benefits. "I couldn't go back to the physical and manual work," he explained, "but I can use computers with all my knowledge and skills. Setting up a business is a completely new challenge for me. It is the best option for me to get off benefits. It's the excitement and thrill of holding my own destiny in my hands."

As to those who started trading, following mainstream trends, there were more men, more who had worked recently and more with some qualifications. But their previous 'out of work' benefits proved no indicator of success and those receiving Disability Living Allowance (DLA, now replaced by Personal Independence Payments – PIP) were only slightly less successful despite having more disabling conditions.

No assumptions.

The accepted mantra at the time was bleak: once on disability benefits for over a year, people were more likely to get their pension or die than work again. In contrast, our holistic guiding principle was never to pre-judge anyone based on their health condition, business idea or potential to succeed. Very many clients had been out of work for years, sometimes decades, but their motivation was still strong.

> *Richard's various health conditions (diabetes, renal failure, a triple heart bypass and a stroke) had stopped him working for about ten years. He still had three six-hour dialysis sessions each week but said, "I like to work and wanted to get back to being*

active. Starting my own business gives me the flexibility I need. It's more than just a job – it's a way of life."

A lasting memory is of the woman who was often too ill to get off her bed. She would lie there, still knitting the goods and garments she sold. To my mind, that's the essential entrepreneurial foundation of an economy.

Limited alternative opportunities.

Cuts following the economic crisis produced a common tale: employers had few vacancies and those with disabilities were at the back of the queue. Employers probably didn't give much weight to PLUs' motivation and courage in trying to get back to work.

One client expressed his frustration: "I was depressed with having to give up a job that I had loved. I applied for jobs but didn't even get replies, let alone interviews."

David described the problems he'd faced when, after 30 years as a qualified joiner, a slipped disc stopped him doing the heavy lifting and bending. "I was warned that, if I carried on, I would need a spinal operation. I had applied for lots of jobs but got nowhere. There were too many others looking for work."

Market failure.

Importantly, and as was still the case in the 2021 Census years later, PLUs who work are more likely to be self-employed than others. Yet, at that time, government-funded business support seemed to ignore this section of their potential market, reporting that less than 1% of their clients were PLUs. They relied on group workshops with little thought of the reasonable adjustments required to include PLUs or the intensive, long term, individual help they might need. The mainstream business language could be off-putting too. Simply talking about 'enterprise, entrepreneurship, limited companies, business turnover' etc was enough to scare our clients off.

Combining professional business experience with flexibility and empathy were the major WFY strengths. John and Nicky's one-to-one home (often) meetings helped with clients' confidence, practical problems and differentiated us from most other business support offerings. Many of the clients would have been daunted by travelling to the uncertain accessibility of a strange corporate setting where the advice, training and information was geared to totally different customers. Add journey difficulties and travel costs to low confidence and there was a recipe for failure.

Nicky and John deserved the praise:

> *"My business adviser does what it says on the tin. She's kept me informed, introduced me to people. I can't give her enough praise really. Out of all the people I've spoken to about this, she's the only one who's been able to help. I would like to say thank you to her." And, "My business adviser has been available every time I've needed him. He is very thorough, went through everything with me. He is easy to talk to, and just what you want when you are trying to set up."*

Outcomes.

We knew from the outset that some clients would eventually decide that self-employment wasn't for them. But their WFY time had often helped them find new confidence, new direction, new goals. They made their own decisions, on their own terms, with far better understanding of possible opportunities. Some found jobs and others started re-training for new careers.

> *"Now I earn a wage and am supporting my family,"* one said. *"It's good not to be relying on money from the State going into my bank." The fundamental difference between being target-driven and working to help a real person succeed.*

Practical problems.

Tapping into ambition was trickier amongst the smaller, dispersed and rural population of the Bolsover district. In those days, public transport could take a couple of hours to reach the basic services and job opportunities in more thriving areas. It was the perfect proving ground for WFY.

With most clients relying on benefits, we offered other practical help with money including the costs of travel in those rural areas, micro-grants and sources of business loans, free/low-cost business cards and computer equipment. While the business loans were available through other organisations, take-up was inevitably low. PLUs with limited funds after, often, lengthy unemployment, had equally limited credit scores and no capital to match-fund grants.

Good results.

Hats off to the thousands who took part and the enormous personal strength of the over 4-in-10 clients changing their lives: 2-in-10 started businesses; nearly the same got jobs, and nearly 1-in-10 started vocational training. It was intensive for most with some 40 to 50 'interventions' spread over some six to nine months each. In 2015, the part-time four-person team had succeeded in achieving all targets, within budget and timescale. More businesses were still trading after 12 months than anyone had expected, and several were starting to recruit their own employees.

> *Martin spoke for many: "Working for yourself gives you independence and you avoid the pressures of working for an employer. It isn't a get-rich-quick scheme but very hard work."*

Clients could overcome huge hurdles: health conditions and deteriorations; government benefit and tax 'officialdom'; finding funds and insurance cover; recruitment processes and finding references; domestic crises and tight finances; both the national and local economic conditions. Those who succeeded were happier and had a more promising future. Many want to work for all the usual reasons but simply can't find a job. Starting their own business was often the only viable alternative, but could depend on the right help.

> *"A big thank you to everyone at Disability Dynamics and John (my business adviser) has been very supportive. I would not have been able to do this without his support. I finally feel like my life is back on track and that I am being a proper role model to my*

children. I am showing them I can still work despite my disability."

The Business Ability ambition.

We'd put self-employment for PLUs firmly on the agenda. Every available media outlet had showcased WFY and our clients through the adverts, thousands of leaflets, radio interviews, press releases and websites, targeting prospective clients and the wider public. We went national too with clients featuring in numerously repeated BBC 'Saints and Scroungers' television programmes.

Each time a programme was repeated, the phone would ring off the hook with calls from other PLUs from across the UK. Who says we PLUs aren't motivated?

The then Business Department was listening to us about new enterprise support policy for PLUs, we'd trained Regional Business Link staff and even ensured equality was covered in their contracts. It was looking positive, but the Work for Yourself adventure ended with DWP's maladministration and injustice over my ATW support. I simply couldn't take the risk of another contract.

But I didn't give up. Having been a non-executive director on the board of HMRC for a couple of years, I spent over another decade supporting one of their working groups concerned with PLUs/customers with additional needs. Whether people are running their own businesses, dealing with other income tax matters, handling an inheritance or more, the department works hard to provide the extra support that PLUs need. It's not perfect but there is ambition.

So what?

Self-employment, starting a business, entrepreneurship – whatever you call it, this sort of work is great for PLUs. We can fulfil our potential, balance work with health and avoid employers' rejection. But PLUs still need business support tailored to our circumstances and aspirations, with cross-departmental help along the way.

CHAPTER 22.

Back to work: the benefits.

We know the macro-stuff. Fewer people claiming out of work benefits means less cost for taxpayers. More people working have more money so spend more to create more economic growth. It's that win-win situation.

But there can be even more benefits at the micro/human -level. These quotes from the WFY projects reveal the better futures that PLUs can achieve.

Regaining self-respect through work.

> *Julie's words reflected the thoughts of many: "Now that I'm off benefits, it's really nice to know that all the money I have is what I've earned myself."*

> *Another said, "Setting up my dog walking business fulfils my ambition to work with animals – and it's good for me as the exercise*

helps my back. Now I just love it and not a day goes by when I don't look forward to work."

And another: "When I look back at the last five years and what I've been through, now it makes me feel fantastic. And the work is just right for me."

One career had ended for Tim when his back condition stopped him working over architectural drawing boards. He reinvented himself as a school teaching assistant and sports trainer. But this came to another halt with government cuts on top of further injury. Undaunted, he said, "Even with reconstructive surgery, my elbow will never be right. But luckily it was my left arm so that I'm still active and can continue coaching – though there is less due to the cutbacks. But I needed an additional way of earning a living and was struggling to find other work. I had done some fence staining before and found I really enjoyed it – it's a different way of getting outside and exercising."

Better health.

Improvements for WFY clients were noticeable, whether they'd just taken part in the programme or progressed to a successful outcome. Most felt their health had improved 'a lot' and many had reduced their times at A&E, GP surgeries and hospital.

> *"I now feel that I can control my illness, and my illness does not control me."*

More positive.

Even more had better quality of life, more optimism and more contact with other people. Not surprisingly for some, a sense of isolation was common after long-term unemployment which could lead to low mood, poor confidence, anxiety and depression. Simply getting up in the morning could become less important, being pro-active waned if every day seemed the same, comfort won out over 'looking the part' when there was no one to see.

> *"I have had depression for nearly half my life which meant that I couldn't work for years.*

Although I'm managing the condition, the medication has difficult side-effects," Julie said. "But this new business means that I get lots of exercise and fresh air, I meet lots of people and get out. Just what the doctor ordered, and I can make an income too. I feel much better now that I know that I am capable of working."

David said, "I had been running my previous business as a keep-fit instructor but, after about 13 years of running six miles every day, my legs were worn out and I couldn't even get upstairs. I had treatment but was told that my working life had finished because I was too young to have replacement knees. So, it was awful being out of work for nearly two years. But then I realised that my health condition need not stop me starting a new business based on my 20 years of hobby micro-light flying. I managed to get some grants for more training so that now I'm a fully qualified flight instructor. I've moved from being down in the dumps with my disability to sitting in my new smart office – it's really uplifting."

David (3) described the situation familiar to so many: "Until 2005, my health was spiralling out of control with nearly fatal consequences. Starting this business has given me something to focus on and helped me to beat the depression. Being off work has been very difficult to handle." Talking about the benefits of self-employment, he continued: "You can take control of your life, and, if you get the chance then do it, as it enables you to regain your self-esteem and your sense of self-worth."

One spoke with professional insight: "Everyone says how much happier I am now. I'm much more optimistic and have been able to reduce my medication. As a trained occupational therapist, I know that keeping busy helps people feel better."

Better home lives.

John expressed some of the benefits: "Having my own business gives me freedom and flexibility for my family life. I may not have the big salary and company car, but I also don't have the stresses and strains of corporate life. Instead, I get to see more of my young son and now have an excellent work/life balance. It's also exciting to make all the decisions, and it's up to me as to how successful the business will become."

Another new entrepreneur saw wider benefits: "The business has given me a new sense of freedom. I am lucky because I have a family that supports me, my wife helps with the paperwork and the children are pleased to see the change in me." New happiness was common: "My business is very satisfying, and I love working and being with my customers. If I make one of them smile and have a laugh, it makes my day."

"I am now working a 30-hour week and managing my health. I am no longer dependant on sickness benefits and have regained my self-esteem. I consider myself to have a better quality of life than before my illness."

"I feel very independent and happy now I am set up in business."

> *"Brilliant support. Would not have been able to do this on my own. Thank you. Has boosted my confidence and self-esteem. Massive improvement in my life."*

Wider impact.

Whole families saw the improvements too.

> *"Now I feel much more confident about the future and can make practical use of my talents with better work/life balance and more time with my family."*
>
> *The work helps my wife too as it reduces her high blood pressure condition."*

So what?

Getting back to work brings much more than money. Feeling better both physically and mentally, having happier families and a brighter future all make life worth living again.

CHAPTER 23.

So what?

These chapters aimed to share key milestones along my PLUs journey. Others will have different ideas and, despite nearly 30 years, I'm still only just a beginner! Here's a summary of those years of learning:

From the start.

Chapter 1.

If you're 16+, there's a 1-in-4 chance you'll be a PLUs too, and the odds get higher after 65.

Chapter 2.

Where you live and how well you did at school are often markers for being a PLUs-in-waiting, for the severity of that life-changing condition and for life expectancy itself. The odds can be stacked from birth.

Chapter 3.

Less education success often means lower/ middle level jobs for PLUs-in-waiting. Health conditions may start to show and short work breaks risk being the first step to job loss. But, good news, around half of PLUs keep working (though different conditions have different chances). Better workplace adjustments might improve the odds.

Chapter 4

Poverty is yet another marker for future PLUs and worklessness. Disadvantaged, deprived communities can be on a downward spiral.

New direction needed?

Chapter 5.

Healthcare can improve both our lives and conditions when the medics see us as real people, not just diagnoses/treatments.

Chapter 6.

Covid was our wake-up call and showed what is possible (albeit narrowly focussed). Better leadership, management, delivery and results are all possible with the right will and urgency. More involvement of the most vulnerable, most at risk in everyday health delivery and emergency planning could benefit everyone. Fingers crossed...

Chapter 7.

Rather than leaving PLUs on the healthcare backfoot, learning from us would benefit everyone.

Chapter 8.

Cross-departmental, top-to-bottom, strategic changes motivated by more than cutting the benefits bill could mean more happy working PLUs, confident employers and a stronger economy too.

Minds matter.

Chapter 9.

Labels (especially the negative ones) change attitudes and behaviour.

Chapter 10.

PLUs often have psychological and mental health consequences on top of our life-changing conditions.

Chapter 11.

Finding the right help can present even more hurdles: accepting the PLUs future; navigating through masses of information; locating the right advice; working through multiple 'systems'. All take their toll.

Chapter 12.

For PLUs to get a fair chance, everyone needs to realise that we're all the same, that disability isn't a lifestyle choice and that we have least power for change.

Carrying on.

Chapter 13.

More control and confidence can give PLUs the courage and commitment to take on the challenge of making a come-back.

Chapter 14.

Doing something/anything is good for mind, body and soul.

The way ahead.

Chapter 15.

Achieving fulfilment of PLUs' potential needn't be difficult: better 'hearts and minds' approach for everyone involved; more focus on employers' responsibilities; recognition that enterprise can be a winner; more cross-departmental working

(DWP, health, education, business, HMRC, justice, ETS, ACAS and probably more).

Chapter 16.

Circumstances beyond our control, rather than choice, can tip PLUs into worklessness. Building on existing relationships with employers is the starting point.

Chapter 17.

With more PLUs out there than most of us probably realise, there are better ways of tapping into all the lost potential. Everyone benefits: PLUs, our communities, wider society and our economy.

On the right track.

Chapter 18.

Successful future back to work ideas will tackle the anxiety, fear, depression and stigma PLUs face. Most life-changing conditions won't go away, but our sense of 'failure' and others' negative reactions can.

Chapter 19.

It's too easy to under-estimate PLUs' potential, motivation and ambition. Likewise, to ignore our skills, insight and capacity to lead and deliver that change. A marriage made in heaven once policymakers realise they don't always know best

Chapter 20.

Designing the 'What' needed by employers and PLUs isn't difficult, but the 'How' of delivery is trickier. Partnerships working together, with shared ambitions, have better chances of succeeding for everyone.

Chapter 21.

Self-employment, starting a business, entrepreneurship – whatever you call it, this sort of work is great for PLUs. We can fulfil our potential, balance work with health and avoid employers' rejection. But PLUs still need business support tailored to our circumstances and aspirations, with cross-departmental help along the way.

Chapter 22.

Getting back to work brings much more than money. Feeling better both physically and mentally, having happier families and a brighter future all make life worth living again.

ANNEX A.

Help to Work Client Journey.

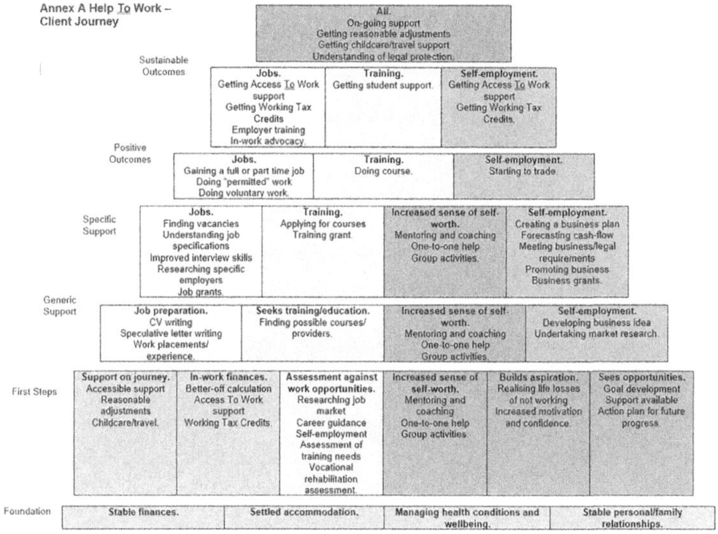

ANNEX B.

Flexicurity Pyramid.

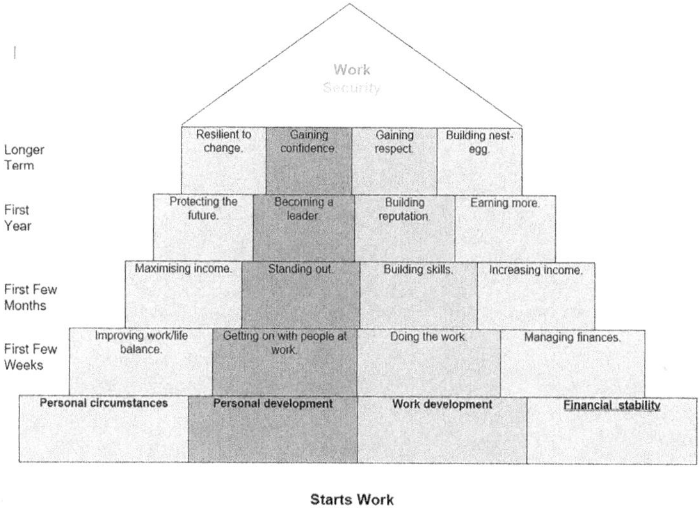

ANNEX C.

Abbreviations and Acronyms.

A&E	Accident & Emergency
AA	Attendance Allowance
ACAS	Advisory, Conciliation and Arbitration Service
AI	Artificial Intelligence
AIS	Accessible Information Standard
ATW	Access to Work
BHS	British Heart Foundation
CA	Carer's Allowance
CAB	Citizens Advice Bureaux
CB	Child Benefit
CQC	Care Quality Commission
CRUK	Cancer Research UK
CV	Curriculum Vitae
DD	Disability Dynamics Ltd
DLA	Disability Living Allowance
DNR	Do Not Resuscitate
DWP	Department for Work and Pensions
EBU	European Blind Union

EHRC	Equality and Human Rights Commission
EPI	Education Policy Institute
ESA	Employment and Support Allowance
ETS	Employment Tribunal Service
GCSE	General Certificate of Secondary Education
GDEP	Gross Domestic Product
GP	General Practitioner
HMRC	His Majesty's Revenue and Customs
IB	Incapacity Benefit
ICO	Information Commissioner's Office
IMD	Indices of Multiple Deprivation
IPPR	Institute for Public Policy Research
IPSO	Independent Press Standards Organisation
IT	Information Technology
JRF	Joseph Rowntree Foundation
JSA	Job Seeker's Allowance
LCP	Lane Clark & Peacock
LFS	Labour Force Survey
NAO	National Audit Office
NEA	New Enterprise Allowance
NHS	National Health Service
OECD	Organisation for Economic Cooperation and Development
ONS	Office for National Statistics
OTT	Over the top!

PIP	Personal Independence Allowance
PLP	Public Law Project
PLUs	People (or Persons) Like Us
PPE	Personal Protective Equipment
RF	Resolution Foundation
SEND	Special Educational Needs and Disability
UC	Universal Credit
UCL	University College London
UN	United Nations
WCA	Work Capability Assessment
WFY	Work For Yourself
WHO	World Health Organisation
Wren	Women's Royal Naval Service

About the author.

A British Royal Navy veteran, blind baker and winner of the international Holman Prize. After 22 years military service, reaching the rank of commander and becoming the first female naval barrister, the author was medically discharged on losing her sight. She created Disability Dynamics, helping people with disabilities to get back to work. She went on to win the Holman Prize for Blind Ambition and has held many senior appointments in the public and voluntary sectors. She's a survivor!

More at: www.pennymelvillebrown.com

By the author.

A Cook's Tour: Baking Blind goes global, also available from Amazon:

https://amzn.eu/d/orM3U6K

Penny used the freshest ingredients in the most eclectic dishes during her tour: red chillies foraged from the Costa Rican jungle; the live chicken destined for the pot in Malawi; disturbingly chewy wood ear mushrooms in China. A unique story with pace and energy, cooking with professional chefs and home cooks (sighted or not), covering six continents, over 100 recipes, links to over 50 demonstration videos plus practical insights into living with disability and surviving a near-death experience.

Printed in Dunstable, United Kingdom

65804397R00151